CODING

CW01080213

A Step By Step Visual Guid   *nd*

Fun Computer Games (*...y ror Kids)*

By

Tommy Wilson

Table of Content

Introduction:

We are living in the digital era, whether we appreciate it or not; therefore, it is essential to adapt change for growth and survival. In such a world, the right approach isn't to keep our children away from the modern gadgets but to train and skill with the digital approach in this fast-paced digital world to put this knowledge and skills in finding new opportunities and exploring possibilities in the upcoming years. This approach can help us prepare to not just survive but excel in the coming future.

Usually, children find interest in games, social media applications, and animations. If your child shows similar interests, then scratch coding could be perfect for them. Scratch coding is a learning experience for children with fun and excitement. Scratch coding will not only help overcome children's fear or hesitation of science but will let them embrace it fully. We can help our children realize the importance of technology through such courses and make it a fun learning experience.

Some groups or community for Scratch are there also wherein parents and different family members can work together for creating further exciting projects. A Gallup survey shows that about 90 percent of parents like computer programming subjects during school for their kids. So, one best idea is that parents and kids should collaborate with each other in creating projects, and both will get benefit from each other. Overall, it's an easy programming language both for parents and kids for creating interactive art, simulation, stories, and games.

Scratch coding is a cool, free tool that could help children in learning to write code without having to type the code out. This means they can learn what coding do and how it is structured without the hassle and frustration of learning syntax.

Engaging in Scratch coding allows kids to experience how programming is like; this could help kids explore their interests and develop skills in various possibilities and opportunities of science and technology. We have seen children how to scratch coding has helped children find their interest in programming. They have been found passionate enough to pursue a degree in computer engineering and then master multiple other languages. Henceforth scratch coding is a healthy appetite for fresh young minds.

Chapter 1: Welcome to Scratch

Scratch was developed for the first time in 2003 at the Massachusetts Institute of Technology. It is now an online tool, but it started out as downloadable software. The National Science Foundation, Google, Microsoft and LEGO Foundation, and various other organizations grant Scratch funds and are completely free.

Scratch's first desktop-only version was developed in 2003 together partnership by Playful Invention Company, Mitchel Resnick, and a consulting firm Montreal-based co-founded by Paula Bonta and Brian Silverman. With no green flag and no labeled categories, Scratch was created with the plan to make kids learn to code; it was started as a basic coding language.

On May 9th, 2013, Scratch 2 was released. Along with various other improvements. The Scratch 2 directly can be downloaded from Scratch's website, along with this offline editor can be downloaded for Linux, Windows, and Mac; however, later, the Linux support was dropped. An unofficial version of mobile from the Scratch forums could also be downloaded.

In 2016 by the Scratch Group for the first time, Scratch 3 was announced. Pre-beta versions "Preview" were released after several public alpha versions from 2013 to 2018. On August 1st, 2018, the beta Scratch 3.0 version for most browsers was released from Internet Explorer.

On January 2nd, 2019 First 3.x Scratch 3.0 version was realized release. The visual programming language Scratch allows Kids to create their own animations, interactive stories, and games. Students learn to think outside the box and creatively, work collaboratively, and reason systematically. Once Scratch is downloaded, the fun part is to create a project you do not need internet access. This is being used in most parts of the world, and the service has been translated into 70 and more different languages. Scratch is used and taught in schools, after-school centers, colleges, and other public knowledge institutions.

Community statistics on the official language website indicate more than 59 million initiatives as of September 2020, shared by more than 58 million people, and approximately 36 million monthly website visits. Scratch derives its name from a method called "scratching" used by disk jockeys, where vinyl records

are manipulated and clipped together to create various sound effects and music on a turntable. The website allows users to combine various media (including graphics, music, and other programmers) in different and creative ways, including scratching, by creating and remixing projects, such as video games and animations.

Scratch is used in several distinct contexts: classrooms, museums, community centers, libraries, and residences. While the targeted consumer age demographic for Scratch is 8-16 years of age, yet it is still used for all ages. For educators and parents, Scratch has been developed. Many surrounding, both physical and interactive, was created through this large outreach. In April 2020, Scratch was ranked in the top 20 of the world's programming languages by Tiobe. There are 50 million projects written in Scratch, according to Tiobe, and one million new projects are added each month.

1.1 Visual programming language

A visual programming language (VPL) in computing is any programming language that helps users construct programs by graphically manipulating program elements rather than textually defining them. A VPL facilitates the programming of visual expressions, spatial text structures, and graphic symbols, used either as syntax or secondary notation components. e.g., many VPLs are based on the principle of 'boxes and arrows' (known as dataflow or diagrammatic programming), where boxes or other screen objects are viewed as entities, linked by relationship-representing arrows, lines, or arcs.

Chapter 2: The scratch Editor

Scratch is considered to develop the basic rules of programming more perceptible and understandable, especially for neophyte young people and children. It has accomplished to perform this without the use of all elements that need in-built adaptation tough. Components that are supposed to encourage motivation and learning have been weighted strongly. Ended projects are possible to make public via Scratch and can be shared with others. Scratch is like playful learning and a topmost significance when a matter is the programming for children.

2.1 The uniqueness of Scratch programming

Scratch is grounded on a graphic operator interface that enables the code typing redundant or complex language syntax. The Foremost and Primary mean is the assistance of neophyte with their initial programming practice. That's why the characteristic of relaxed useableness always bears preference over the functional variability. Despite these limitations, Scratch, however, bears some significant properties of conventional paradigms of programming as the given list delineates. These are:

- Visual: Entire elements of Scratch are shown via a coherent graphical representation, for Example, program command through the image blocks. These can be easily put together and inserted additionally through drag-and-drop.

- Object-oriented: Along with scratch programming, no classes or an inheritance system are there. Along with objects like polymorphism (items can undertake different types of data) or data encapsulation (controlled approach up to data through defined interfaces), Scratch, however, determines the features of the object – concerning the concept of programming.

- Imperative: Several scripts for programming with a scratch that is accessible to you track the imperative programming paradigm. Thus, instruction orders define in which order the action type should be performed.

- Event-oriented: Each Script which you practice in a scratch project initiates immediately as the event well-defined in its header blocks. By using the 'Wait Until' block, the project loading can also be deferred until the specific event occurs.

- Parallelism – supporting: The division of the programs of the computer into separate sub-components that differentiate the code of parallel programming is maintained from the outset in Scratch.

2.2 Tutorial of Scratch: program learning

One of the best sayings, i.e., practice makes perfect' is also applicable to the coding of Scratch. However, the encoding project gives the hurdles for the entrance that are obviously less than the classic programming languages. It certainly requires some time to acquaint one's with and adopt the available blocks and the user interface. In the given scratch tutorial, we depict to you that how you can make your self-registered on the scratch platform and then familiarized with all the user interface's core components. In order to draw the conclusion, we elucidate the programming by using a definite example of a project with Scratch.

To commence a scratch project, to set up an account is not mandatory for you generally. Simply you can also approach the scratch platform by initiating your desired browser and by clicking the button of 'Start Creating' for joining the great scratch community and enabling to share the games and videos etc. with others. However, upon completion, a user account will be required. That is why it expresses the registration sense.

For creating the user account, just click the 'Join Scratch' button. Then enter your favorite username and a secured passcode in the consequent menu:

You can freely choose your username (if not assigned already) and passcode to the Scratch account.

Following the 'Next' button clicking, you will be required to mention personal information such as your date of birth and country of origin. In the final step to conclude the registration, you will be required to mention an effective email address and then click on the 'Set Up Your account" button.

You will then be registered automatically. Also, you will find a link in your email inbox, by which you can activate features for commenting and publishing on programmed projects of Scratch.

Learn the Scratch: Checklist of user interface

If you have set up your user account and logged into the profile, there are various options available, and by the upper menu bar, these can be selected.

When you click on the "Account button", you will be able to manage personal profile, password, location setting, email address, and also the overview of your active project. Additionally, you will be able to log out as well.

Close to the Account button, there will be two other buttons for the instant repossession of project (file icon) and received messages (Envelope icon).

Other than the hidden menu, available items have the following features:

- **Develop**: The web project's central components of the Scratch are the 'graphic development environment' that you can launch through the" Development tab". With the assistance of a web editor, you can run all the scratch applications into the browser directly.

- **Explore:** You can call up the other user's project in this category. You, by doing so, not only playback but can see all the scratch programming also. Similar types of projects are collective in 'studio'.

- **Ideas:** This section allows you to approach the various guide and tutorials that help you in developing your particular projects when dealing with brainstorming. Also, you can find a link to redirect the downloading of the scratch app (macOS, Windows, Android, Chromes) that allows you to program exclusive of an internet connection.

- **About Scratch:** If you go to the "About Scratch "menu, you will be taken to a page of general information regarding the Scratch project'. You will discover links in other things, for supporting data for teachers and parents, and also the FAQ section and the tips as well.

Understanding the Scratch Editor: this is how Scratch coding works

The development environment of Scratch is evocative of a building block of the homepage that doesn't offer the block-nature of the accessible Script so astonishing. Additionally, these scripts, that form most of the functioning components. Sounds and costumes can also be added to a project so that you can implement or manage through scripts. The script selection can be enhanced by clicking on the "**Add Extension".** For Example, text-to-speech feature or with crayon code for recording the video.

Costumes: Bring figures and objects to life

With Scratch whatsoever, you would want to program – animation or video, a game, or maybe a simple comic even; for your story, figures and other things are the vital building blocks. You can choose and also integrate numbers of graphics below the **'Costumes" tab** into **your project.** Select from the **image options, by hand draw the object** or **import** the locally stored graphics. Also, you have the option of captivating a **photo** as your device has a camera.

Figures or objects in different poses, later on, present the option of causing the sequences of motions.

If you select a costume, then you can customize it at your desire. To process this, choose the desirable object in the **left-side menu** (where any time you can delete it just by clicking on the Recycle Bin icon) and use the editor tools available to you. For Example: eliminate some detail by using an eraser, change colors, wrap the object, and add text.

A conversation of graphics into a vector or raster is possible also. You can also express the **costume name** in the **'Costume'** pitch, to which the particular scripts need as reference value later.

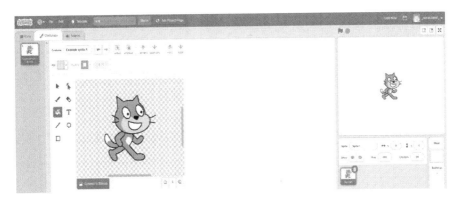

We have accustomed figure appearance in this tutorial example of Scratch, by filling its color.

You will find a button **"Choose a Backdrop"** on the window's right margin. By which you can determine the background image of your project. Scratch offers a choice of stock images or import your own image or paint your background graphic.

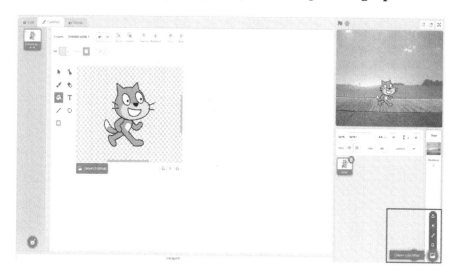

By using a script, you can switch or move the background in Scratch, just like with figures and objects.

Background Music and Sound

The suitable soundtrack is as important as figures and objects for many creative projects. You manage and implement all sounds through the menu of the same name when programming with Scratch. On the one hand, with the graphic elements, you have a selection of pre-created sounds of Scratch available for the purpose that you can approach through

"Choose Sound". The option is present for recording or importing the sounds provided, on the other hand, when you connect a microphone.

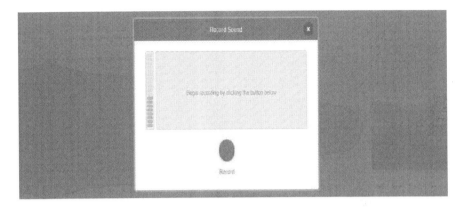

A new scratch sound recording will start as early you click the record button.

In the left-side menu, the chosen Sound can be inserted just by clicking the matching thumbnail and edit in various ways. For Example; In other things, you can cut out the selected sequences, increase or decrease the playing speed or adjust the volume at your will. Because of the integration of Sound with the use of scripts in the scratch projects, every Sound also needs an inimitable name that will be assigned in the "Sound" field.

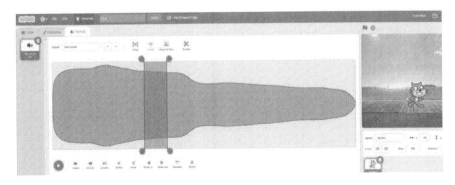

If you are willing to edit the selected part or to cut the specific sequences, hold the left button of the mouse and select these from a desirable starting point and drag out the selected screen toward the end of an anticipated endpoint.

Scripts; the crux of Scratch coding

It is mandatory to practice the handling of Scratch scripts for successful programming with Scratch. Behind these scripts, the actual codes are generated automatically as early as the available blocks will be dragged into the project – irrespective of either it is an operator, event, variable, or a function. You can focus on the insertion of relevant scripts with specific values and the particular sound components and graphics.

For the entire pre-created scripts, a brief description is there to delineate the functions they bear. If you are willing to apply a script in the project, just drag out the respective **block** simply into the middle editor window. Defined options or values can be seen directly on the block and also selected there or typed directly. Such a new script should directly recommend a pre-inserted script, then attach the matching block simply as you like if you are putting the puzzle together.

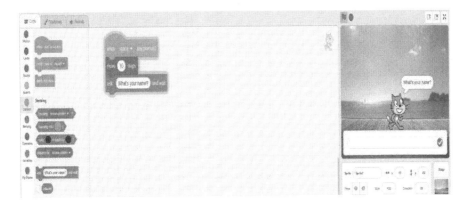

In the current version, you can review your scratch project in the preview window at any time, and for test purposes, playback the applied sequences.

Chapter 3: Building & running a script

In your desire internet browser, Scratch is opened by visiting its site. To save the work, you are required to make a free account of Scratch by clicking the "Join Scratch" option in the right top corner. Once the account is set up and then login by clicking the "Create" button of the homepage in the left top corner. This will lead to the editor screen project.

Focus on Fig 1, and then you will see Scratch's five main areas, i.e., the Script Area, the Block Menu, the Stage, the Grey color Toolbar, and the Sprite Zone.

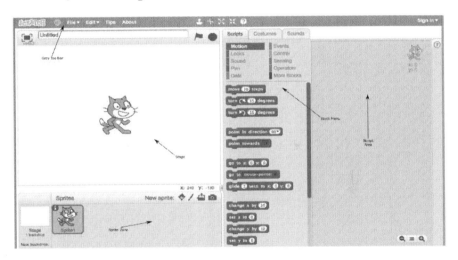

Figure No. 1. The workspace of Scratch consists of 5 areas. The Grey color toolbar is on the screen top.

Big is the Stage, and the white box consists of the Cat. In the screen middle is the Block Menu. The area of the Script is also big, and there is a grey color box on the screen right side. In the end, there is a Sprite zone at the screen's bottom and left corner.

Look at the Stage – the large white color box on the screen's left side. Currently, you have 1 Sprite. Every time the Cat (default) will appear when you open the new project on Stage. Allow it to move crosswise to the Stage, just like in figure 2; the Cat's doing.

Figure No. 2. You are about to write to a program that'll allow you to move the Cat in the arrow's direction. You can do this by writing the program that will tell the PC to move the Cat, and the manner of your writing a program is blocks clicking & dragging from the menu of the block to the area of the Script in Scratch.

Steer to the Menu of the Block to start:

1. Click the "Event" word to go to the "Event" block menu.

2. When the Flag is clicked

3. Press the mouse button, and to any space, the block is dragged in the script area.

4. Leave the mouse.

Fig no 3, you will see the way which block will make from the menu of the block to the area of the Script.

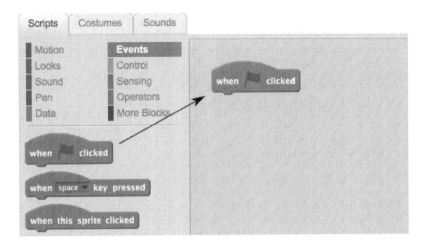

Figure No. 3. To initiate the programming, just drag & drop out the blocks from the menu of the block to the area of the Script. You will now be asked that to start your program when above the Stage, the Green color Flag is clicked.

After clicking the green color Flag, you tell now your will that what you like to do.

Move the Cat

On the Stage, upright is the Cat that is somewhat boring. So, let move the Cat. Steer back to the Menu of the Block to mention the next steps in the program:

1. Click the "Motion" word for changing to the block menu Motion.

2. Then click on the move ten steps

3. Press the mouse button and to any space, drag the underneath block of Flag clicked in the area of the Script.

4. Move the block ten steps next to see the white color space form in the bottom when Flag is clicked. White space can be seen in fig 4.

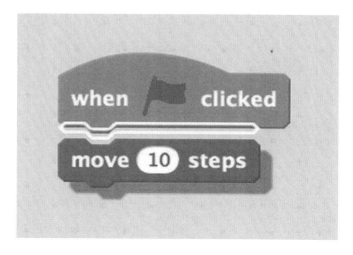

Figure No. 4.

When among the two blocks, the white color space is shown, then they are ready to grab together when releasing the mouse.

The mouse is released so that the new block is snapped to the existing. Two blocks can be seen together in fig 5.

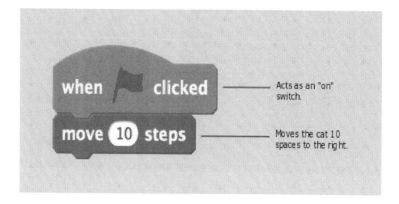

Figure No. 5. These two blocks work jointly for making a little program that mobilizes the Cat ten steps.

You can check the program by clicking the green color Flag over the Stage. The slight cat movement to the right can be seen.

Fix it if the Cat does not move

What will happen if your Cat doesn't move by clicking the green color Flag on the Stage? This means that the two blocks are not snapped together in your program. If the block of "Move 10 steps" is in the area of the Script, but it didn't touch the block of when Flag clicked, then again click the block of Move 10 steps and also drag it to When Flag clicked block unless the white color strip is shown. The mouse is then released to get both blocks grabbed into place.

When every time clicking the green color Flag over the Stage, the ten steps move of Cat should be seen.

Block Changing

Some blocks can be dragged & dropped, but in others, spaces are there where other blocks can be added. Select an object from the drop menu/type a new set of values. By typing some new value, the block of "Move 10 steps" can be altered.

Usually, for the block, we use the already present name. For Example: to reading Move 100 steps, you change this block after it is still listed in the instructions; move ten steps. Changes that are made by you to block, using the typing or via the dropdown menu, will be remembered by Scratch. Thus, there could be a little difference between my screen versus the manner of appearance of the block. In the guidelines, if you look at a block but unable to find the same block in the menu of the block, then check the named block similar to it. We are using the block default name, but there is possible that you see the exact block having the different values enumerated in the dropdown menu or type-able space.

Value changing from 10-100 steps:

1. Click the white color bubble on Move 10 step

2. Remove the 10.

3. Type the 100 figures.

In figure no 6, a new value can be seen in the mid of the block of Move 10 step.

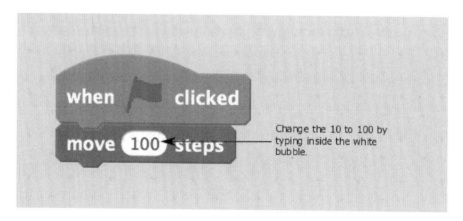

Figure No. 6. Many blocks in the Scratch can be altered by adding new info or selecting from the dropdown menu.

When the green color Flag is clicked over the Stage, the Cat can be seen taking across the screen, an enormous step because now, at a time, in place of 10 spaces, she is moving 100 spaces.

Fix the Runaway Sprites

On the green color Flag, click much time so the Cat will be disappeared from the Stage right side, but only the tail and legs will be shown. You don't need to be worried about that because the Cat can get back again to the Stage left side, and also, it can again walk across. In order to position it, any sprite you can move over the Stage where you want to start it. Just click on the Cat & drag it to the Stage's left side by holding the mouse meanwhile. Let the mouse go off when the Cat comes at the point where you like to begin it.

Every time you need to move the Cat, what you need to do is to click just the green color Flag. To keep proceeding the exact step, again and again, you can set up your program also unless the program gets to stop.

Step Continuation

You require a plethora of space if you want to program the Cat to walk ahead until the end of the program. So, by clicking & dragging to some new place, move the Cat on the Stage. (For more information, see Fix the Runaway Sprites).

To move the Cat continuously just with one click:

1. Alter the value in the block of the "Move 10 steps" (or block of Move 100 steps now) back from 100-10.

2. Click the "Control" word to shift to the block menu of Control.

3. Click then Forever, which looks like the head of an alligator that is suitable because you are going to make the block of the "Move 10 steps" shallow.

4. Press the mouse button and drag out the block in the Script Area beneath the block of the When Flag Clicked.

5. "Forever" block is moved next to the block of "When flag clicked" to see "bottom white on the block of the "Move 10 steps" will be under the block of Forever. For a moment, you may be unable to see it.

6. The mouse is released, So the block of "Forever" grabbed the block of "When Flag Clicked." The block of "Move 10 steps" is inside the block of "Forever."

Analyze the Script. Are three blocks in the exact sequence as figure no: 7?

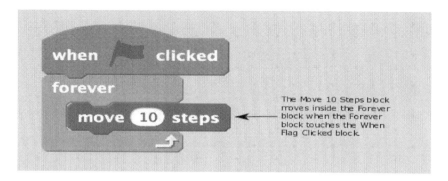

The Move 10 Steps block moves inside the Forever block when the Forever block touches the When Flag Clicked block.

Figure No. 7.

Sometimes in Scratch, even one block goes inside another block.

To test your program, click on the green color Flag over the Stage and look at the sliding Cat across a screen smoothly.

Fix-It: Out of Order Blocks

If you are facing trouble while sliding blocks in an accurate sequence, discard the block of "Move ten steps" for a while just by dropping back within the area of the Block general Menu, and put the block of "Forever" into the place. Then open the menu of "Motion" block again and snap a new block of "Move ten steps" and skid it within the block "Forever."

The block of "Forever" cast the program within the block for running indeterminately.

It moves the Cat 10 steps in this case until you halt the program via the red color stop sign button close to the green color Flag.

On the Stage, you may have further than 1 Sprite. Let place the 2nd Sprite to watch what occurs when you commence adding the number of sprites to the project.

New Sprite Addition

See your screen's left bottom corner, i.e., your spirit zone. It is the place where all the sprites & backdrops will be live. You made them once. This is the space also where you switch between the Sprites so that you also can program everyone. The sprite zone consists of cat sprite (default), which initiates with the Scratch projects (new projects), and that is visible in fig 8.

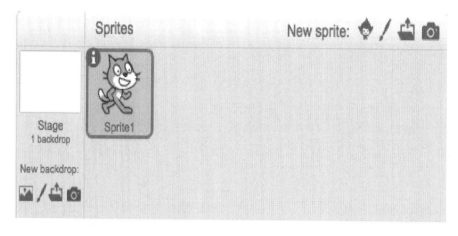

Figure No. 8.

Your entire sprites will be in the Sprite Zone. You can fill that area with your makings that you can draw in Art Editor. The new Sprite is now borrowed from a Sprite menu of Scratch(built-in).

For adding the new Sprite:

1. Click on the icon head-shaped close to the Sprite zone top and on the right side of the "New Sprite" word, as in fig no 9.

2. By double-clicking on a picture, choose the cluster of bananas sprite

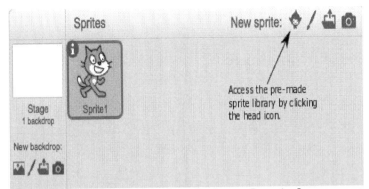

Figure No. 9. The icon head-shaped switches you to a preformed sprite library.

In the Sprite zone, see the new bananas sprite

In your sprite zone, two sprites can be seen as in fig 10. On the Stage, both sprites can also be seen.

Figure No.10. Now there are two sprites in your Sprite zone,

Currently, around the Sprite, there is a blue box. When in Scratch you write up a script, you are programming the Sprite. You will be programming the bananas if you have written right now the Script because of the blue color box that's in a Sprite zone around the bananas. To make certain that you proceed to Cat programming, not the bananas, click the Cat. As in figure 11, the blue color box should be now around the Cat.

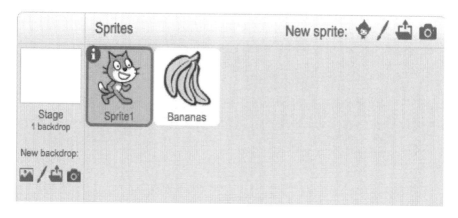

Figure No.11. In the Sprite Zone, the blue color box is around the Sprite of the Cat, meaning the programming will be on Cat.

Fix-It: Bananas mobility in place of the Cat.

The huge mistake that scratchers make is the programming on the wrong Sprite. Overall, the program is highly frustrating, and realize that by clicking the green color Flag, the bananas are programmed in order to move towards the Cat, in place of moving the Cat towards bananas. Avoid this type of mistake always by making sure that prior to beginning the programming, the blue color box is near the accurate Sprite in a Sprite zone.

Now you are ready for writing up the last Script. By the existing Script dragging back within the Menu of "Block", clear the "Script Area". By clicking on the block of the "When Flag

Clicked" and slide on every block connected to that in the meantime, this can be done.

Unknown Blocks Trying

The thing regarding Scratch is the no susceptibility of breaking. The bad thing that can occur is the messing up of the program on which you are working. (Don't be worried; Once the programs become complex, you have the choice to create a copy of the project. So, without messing with your project, you can experience). It means you can try each block to analyze what occurs when within the place it is snapped by you. And, you can play with values and dropdown menus.

To begin, use the different block of the "Event" to start your project:

1. Click the "Events" word to go to the block of the Events menu.

2. Then "When Space key Pressed" is clicked.

3. Press down the mouse & the block is dragged to any Script Area space.

4. Let go of the mouse

5. Select another option like the "A" letter by clicking the dropdown menu on the block

Whenever a small triangle is shown on the block, it indicates the rope down menu in fig 12.

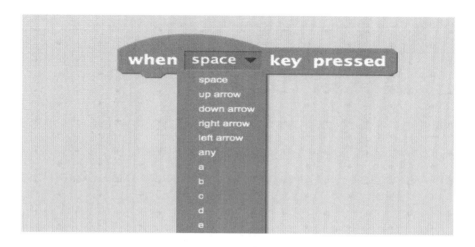

Figure No. 12. Multiple options are given to programmers by a dropdown menu.

Now by selecting the new block, peruse the Script. Do you like to move your Cat around? Then visit the "Menu of motion" and select the block of the "Turn 15 Degrees". Do you wish the Cat to meow? Then visit the "Menu of Sound" and select the block of "Play Sound Meow". Which program can be made by you by clicking & dragging the blocks into the place? You want to try to make your Script and set up the option in the block of the "When Space key Pressed" and snap to it one/two other blocks? To initiate the program, click the key that you designed in the "dropdown menu". For Example: If you specified the Space bar for it, then press the space key to initiate the program.

Well done, you have created the first Script. It is so simple to use Scratch. For creating complex games, your programs will be even longer. By dragging & dropping the blocks within the area of the Script, you will be able to create all these programs.

Chapter 4: What are programs

A common programming word that can be used as both a noun and a verb is a program. Executable software that operates on a machine is a program (noun). It is similar to a script but is also much bigger in size and does not require running a scripting engine. Instead, a program consists of a compiled code that can run directly from the machine's operating system.

Web servers, word processors, e-mail clients, video games, and machine utilities are examples of programs. "These programs are sometimes referred to as" computer programs "applications and can be used synonymously with" software programs. "Programs generally have a .EXE file extension on Windows, while Macintosh programs have an APP extension on them. This involves designing a software application, while "application" is used as a noun. Programmers, for instance, build programs by writing code that tells the machine what to do. The functions and commands that the compiler writes are referred to collectively as source code. When the programming is completed, it compiles the source code file or files into an executable program.

4.1 Programs Versus Apps

When the iPhone was introduced by Apple, they propagated the terminology of "App", but the program and an app (application) are similar things. Nowadays, lots of people think about an "app" as the application of Apple smartphones, tablets, or computers. The program is considered as something runs by the windows computer.

4.2 Scripts Vs. Program

When the program is made, it is compiled into the understandable language of the computer. The program is compiled once; it doesn't require another program as long a computer needs the platform and an operating system to run. In contrast, the Script is composed and requires an interpreter to interpret the Script into the understandable form of the computer. The Script will not be run on a computer without the aid of an interpreter. However, a script installed once is able to run without the necessity of rewriting on any platform. For further information and scrutiny of the advantages and disadvantages, read our Script terms.

What types are the program files?

It must be a processable file. It ends with the extension of .PIF .exe and .com for those software programs that run on Microsoft windows. The program runs by the processing of these files and permits them to be used on a computer. A program on the Apple Macintosh computer ends with the extension of .APP.

Examples of computer programs

Today, millions of various types of programs for phones,

computers, and other devices. Few examples and the relevant program categories are given below.

What is the program's purpose?

Without programs (application software), a computer is able to operate with system software (operating system) but is unable to perform anything else. The program provides the ability to the user computer to do special tasks. Such as, you need to install the browser for internet surfing on a computer. A browser is actually the program that guides the computer about the visit, web page navigation, and a display. The computer is unable to internet surfing without the use of any browser.

What are the fundamental roles of a program?

The basic function of the program is varied and depends on the program's type. Such as browser program browses the internet. Word processor functions in view, create and edit the documents. For a special faction (task) program is designed. Simply we can say that a word processor program is only able to create documents, but it is not capable of browsing the internet.

Are games programs too?

Yes, of course, games are also the programs. But for the purpose of differentiation of leisure activity than the productive targets, these are named as "games," not the programs. As a program's category part, there are sub-categories of games like MMO,

RPG, and FPS. For instance, Quake lies in the FPS sub-category.

Is Microsoft Windows the program?

No, it is not a program. It's all versions. They are known as the operating system.

Which one was the first program?

The very first software program was formed by Tom Kilburn that was used in an electronic memory. This calculated the highest factor of integer 218=262,144 and was processed successfully at the University of Manchester, England, on 21 June 1984. The computer was named Small scale Experimental Machine (SSEM), then called "Manchester Baby". Now, this event is celebrated extensively as the birth of software.

4.3 6 Basic Concepts of coding

There are six fundamental concepts of coding that is helpful for you in mastering the coding basics in any language.

Data Flow

Prior to initiating the writing of your code first line, you are required to recognize the flowing way of data via program and what is required to happen all the way. A better understanding is needed in the entire process that by the user which kind of data be input and retrieved from the pre-existing source of data such as the databases. You are required to perceive the way of data manipulation, and the program selection is anticipated and the conditions upon which these sections should be made.

Data Types

Most computer programs cannot perform any useful thing without some specific data type. Basically, there are 3 data types. 1st type is the string that manipulates text. 2nd type is numerical data, which is used for the algorithms and calculation. 3rd is a catch-all that is used for any other data type such as Boolean values.

Syntax

In the rules, it is the pre-baked that administers the way of code processing by different languages. Codes in one language may have a completely different meaning in other languages. That difference sometimes may be small as the words are written in order. You may be indulged long before within niceties such as ruby versus merits of pythons; you need a strong command that how the syntax works. For new coders, one of the difficult challenges could be the "Learning to spot syntax error". Many sophisticated coding environments comprise tools; fortunately, that will be helpful in finding the errors.

Control Structures

Languages are derived with their peculiar built-in rules. But to perceive the way of processing the programs for a machine, you need to define the other rules also by yourself, and they are called control structures. These control structures define the conditions; certain things occur in the program. Also, these guide a program about the command execution and to make the choices. For instance, If you want to write a point of the "sale" program and command for the only receipt on customer request, y you are required to enter the control structures that will direct the program to print only a receipt upon receiving the pre-defined response from a user.

Functions

Most computer programs process the same directives multiple times. Different functions let you repeat the instructions, irrespective of typing those instructions each time, which needs to be processed in the program. By giving a name to the set of instructions, functions work that can be then referenced later in the instruction's place in a program. Some programming languages comprise libraries as built-in functions and some completely rely on the functions.

Variables

Variables are just like the functions, but the variables point refers to the piece of data instead of a group of instructions. At the start of your program, it needs to be declared. So that about the action, it is known to the program while facing them in the code. That makes you reference the data in a code which is not stored yet in the system. Such a thing is most advantageous for the data which needs to be input by the user.

Few coding languages are too identical, while rests have their peculiar syntax and rules. Learning these fundamental concepts can deliver you the set of transferable skills that could be fruitful for you throughout your entire career.

Chapter 5: The basics of Scratch

With time, Scratch's team will launch the updated version of Scratch for Windows, Linux, or Mac OS X.

5.1 Installing the Scratch

For using Scratch, there are two ways:

1. Install the Scratch on your computer (it is free of cost). Download will take a few minutes. Once it is downloaded, then there is no need for an internet connection, and you and your child can save their creative work on home PC.

Or

2. Use Scratch online (it is Free of cost also). You or your kid can use Scratch's online editor, by the access of internet connection from home PC. Go to the website www.SCRATCH.mit.edu and press the "JOIN SCRATC H' button. You will need to create an account for your kid with a valid username and passcode. For verification and activation of the account, an email address will also be required. All these will be set up within a few minutes. Then Your kid can access his Scratch account from any computer. On any website, while selecting the username for your kid, always try a fun name or nickname. Also, make certain while setting an easy password that your kid can memorize that. Lots of helpful hints and tips, and some sample projects are there for your kid in Scratch, which is helpful in creating his own fantabulous masterwork.

If your kid is younger and he feels it as expended, for that, there is Scratch Junior application that can be downloaded from all App stores freely. This is quite easy and joyful to use for youngers with the age of 5 to 7 years.

5.2 How to: Save a Project

The project is saved automatically when the Scratch editor detects the changes in content. However, if someone is willing to save the project manually, time may be there. Such as to make sure simply the saving of content or to updating the thumbnail. The ability to save a project in any situation is an upright practice in the prevention of losing data in any unpredicted situations.

For saving the project to the online editor, there are two ways. In order to save it, a more common way is clicking the "Save Now" button that is located at the right corner of the editor.

You can also save the project by clicking the "File" button in the toolbar. From the drop-down menu, then click the "Save Now".

You can also thirdly save the project, i.e., by pressing the CTRL+S or Cmd+S on a Mac on your PC keyboard.

When the "Save" button shows the "Project saved" and disappears, then the project will be saved successfully. The project, which is in the progress of saving on the server, will show the "Saving project," and it will also display a throbber close to the "Saving project" text.

If the project doesn't save successfully, a window will be displayed that will notify the user that the project couldn't be saved. The user can select the chance of saving the project again in a window by clicking the "Try again" button or can select the download option as a File just by clicking the "download".

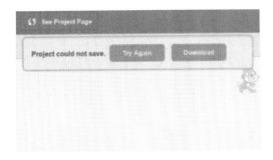

A window is depicting that an error has occurred while attempting to save besides the options which a user can choose.

Projects will save automatically save while working occasionally.

5.3 Download a Project

Downloading in some cases could be useful for users, such as the backup of the contents of their project to their storage.

Click the "File" option in the toolbar to download the project. Click the "Save to your computer" option from the drop-down menu. This will start downloading to the "downloads" folder on your PC. Your project will be saved as a ".sb3" file that can be uploaded again later onto the original file.

When there is no Wi-Fi connection or for some other reasons the project doesn't be saved, then to download the project, there will be a popup option.

5.4 Upload a Project

Caution: Projects can't be combined. All the project's content will be replaced with the files by uploading the project.

For uploading the previously downloaded project, steer to that project whose contents are to be substituted. (create a blank project to replace the file if it was created without internet access). Click the "File" from the drop-down menu, then click 'load from your computer'. Following the selection of an authentic file, click "Open". The project will be loaded on the Scratch editor. The file size of the project is maxed as a ".json file" at 5 megabytes. Download the projects to analyze that how big is .json file and also change the ".sb3" extension to ".zip".

5.5 Bugs

In Scratch, there are various notable bugs. Some may be just graphical, and some make the text missed. Some might affect the coding and some extra display things.

Current Bugs

The wrong Font Bug

In the paint editor of Scratch 3.0, the Sans Serif font is displayed as the larger font. This bug cause is unknown, and there is no available solution. But the work is to use the Japanese, Korean or Chinese fonts instead because they look identical to the Sans Serif font.

No Last Post Bug

When in May 2017, the spammer was active, the "last post" field close to the subforum description on some occasion was missing. Although he died after, forum changes appeared to fetch it back later. The main cause of this happening remains unknown.

Disappearing Comment Bug

In Scratch 3.0, the majority found that this bug causes to do not show projects, studio comments, and profile when trying to view.

When sometimes, while clicking the message for comment, the comment section is not loaded. That results in the failure to reply, view, report, or delete the comment. Do a firm refresh to fix that.

Fix the Bugs

Disabled Keyboard Bug

In scratch 2.0 only, this bug was seen that caused not to react upon keys pressing that influenced the project in the way that scratchers cannot program because of this. By which most of the blocks that need the word typed into them to work efficiently. Only with Firefox, this bug was seen. Currently, there is no way to fix that permanently, but it had been observed that by clicking outside the Scratch (like address bar) fixed transitionally.

Semicolon Glitch

Semicolon Glitch is also a bug that displays the semicolon at the left bottom of each side. Since it has been fixed, but this bug has been brought several times again on April Fool Day.

Disappearing Text Bug

Disappearing text bug is the text that disappears in some projects. It has been seen in the blocks with drop-down menus or with written text inside. Only some text disappears in some cases, but all text disappears in some cases. This bug has been fixed, and although it is also reported that this bug has been seen again in Scratch 2.0. For a few years, it has not been observed.

Variables Not Fully Hiding

Sometimes variables do not disappear completely from the Stage even make hidden through the checkbox near to its name in Scratch 2.0. The exact reason is unknown, but it is thought that backdrops or instant switching costumes are responsible for that.

White Text

In Scratch 2.0, the website of the project is loaded in Firefox with black text that appears white. The reason is unknown, but it is speculated it is identical to the "Disabled keyboard Bug".

Speech Bubbles with Empty Space at the Bottom

Sometimes, there is extra space at the bottom of a speech bubble.

When switching to full screen in Scratch 2.0, the exterior of the speech bubble became amplified to accurate volume, but relative to the bubble, the text seemed a little smaller. Consequently, the speech bubble was slightly big as compared to it is considered to be. This happens only with a large speech bubble or speech bubbles having lots of text.

A debugging workflow

It is a type of workflow. A professional-level programmer can use that If he is notified of an error by the user in a program.

Duplicate the error, so that they can see it for themself

Trace the reason that is causing that, make the collective logical thinking and testing

By updating of code, fix the problem

The study from such previous experience in order to avoid it happening again

In the process, there could be loops because the fixation of one error may unleash another.

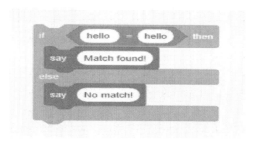

Chapter 6: Making it move

Selecting a Sprite then Moving in all directions.

In comparison to Microsoft Excel or word Scratch runs in a quite different way. When the Scratch program is run, actually, you're running a Squeak program having a Scratch image. The visual environment appears a bit different in contrast to windows XP. When on a different operating system like Linux, OS X, Windows, you Squeak and run the Scratch, the appearance and Scratch feels the same.

The layout of Scratch

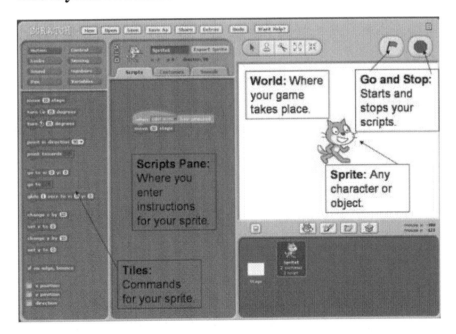

Step No. 1: Choosing the Sprite

In the game, an object or character is the Sprite. It can stay still and can move also. Select the Sprite that can move on the screen

1. Open the Scratch

a. Go on that folder where the "Scratch" is copied.

b. Double click on the icon of Scratch.

2. Opening screen will appear as below

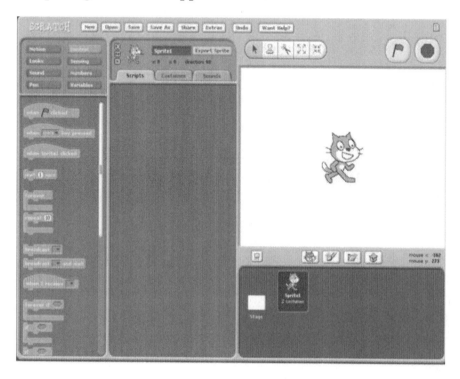

3. Click the Tab "Costumes."

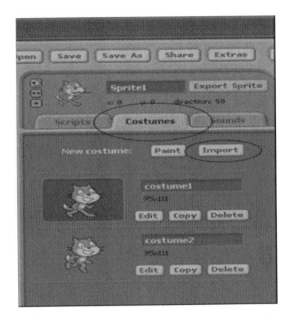

4. Click on "Import."

5. A Folder (Things, Animals, People) is selected now.

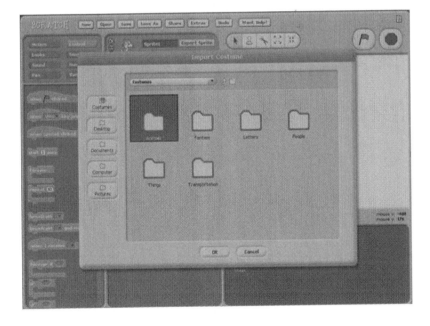

6. By Double Click Choose the Sprite.

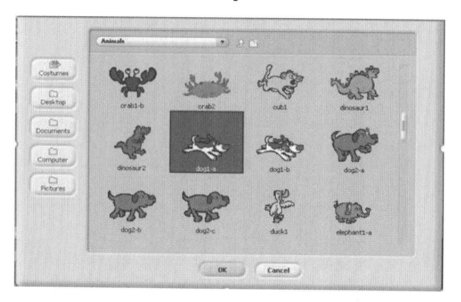

Step No. 2: Moving the Sprite in four directions (Up, Down, Right, Left)

By themselves, Sprite can't do something. The action of Sprite comes from the window of the Script. Actually, these are the instructions for the Sprite that what will they be doing. Fromthe pain of tile, you drag the instructions into the pane of Script. like a puzzle, these tiles fit for creating instructions.

7. Click the Tab "Script."

8. To the right side, you like to move the Sprite. Click on the button"Control."

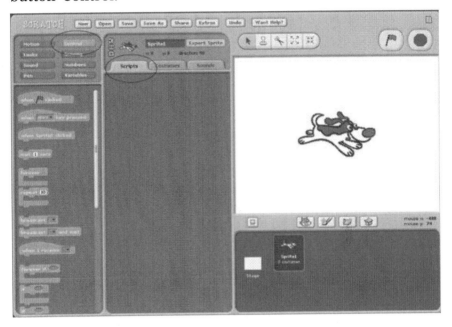

9. Left-click & hold when pressed the 'space' command and move to the window of Script.

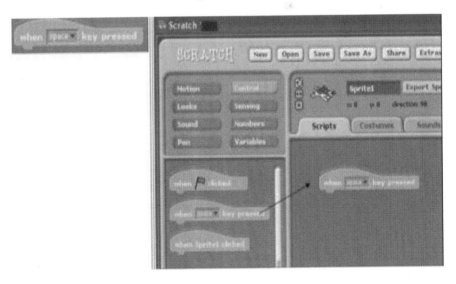

10. Click the 'space' word, then the "right arrow" is selected.

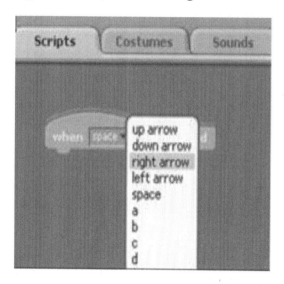

11. Click the button "Motion", then drag "90, point in direction" over the window of the Script.

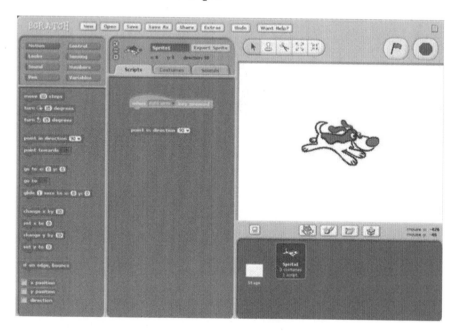

12. The tile "point in direction" is connected to the command "When 'right arrow' pressed".

13. Click the tile, "Move ten steps, then drag over the window of the Script.

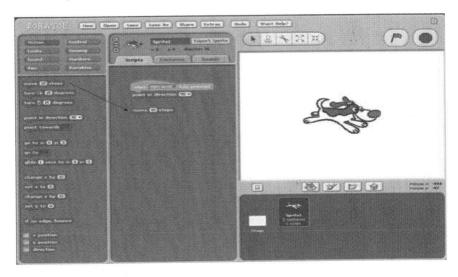

14. "Move ten steps" is connected to the tile "point in a direction."

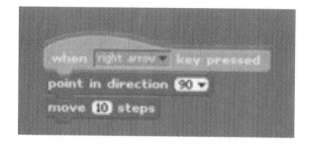

15. On the computer, the right arrow is pressed, and see the Sprite moving to the right.

16. Sprite moving to the left by dragging the tile "When space pressed" to the window of the Script.

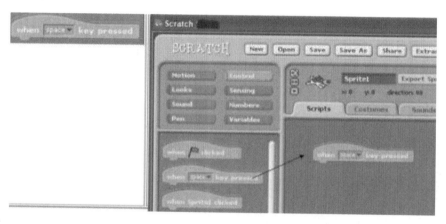

17. Drag "90, point in direction" over the window of the Script. Connect it to the tile of "When 'space' pressed."

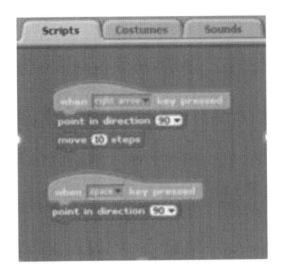

18. To "left arrow" change the space. To '-90' change the '90' for making left the face of the Sprite.

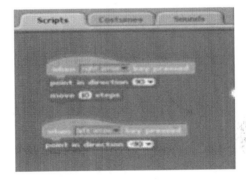

19. The tile "Move ten steps" is dragged to the window of the Script and then connected to the script 'left arrow.'

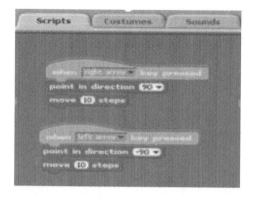

20. The left arrow now will work. The icon "flip left-right" is clicked for making the Sprite facing in the right direction.

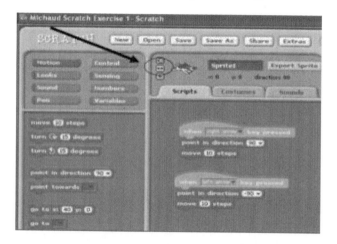

21. Making the Sprite move down by dragging and connecting the tiles below.

i. "When 'space' pressed

ii. "90, point in a direction."

iii. "Move ten steps."

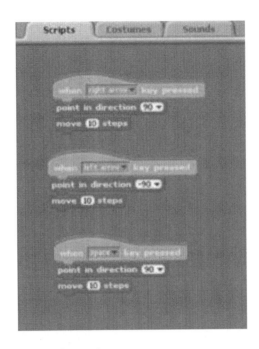

22. To down Set the direction.

i. To 'down arrow change' space.'

ii. To '180', '90' is changed.

23. Set the direction to down:

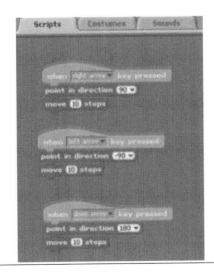

24. The down arrow will work now.

25. Move up the Sprite. The tiles below are dragged and connected.

i. "When 'space' pressed

ii. "90, point in a direction."

iii. "Move ten steps."

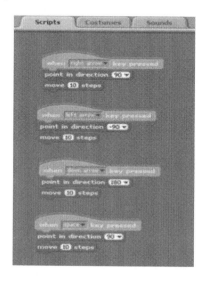

26. To up, set the direction.

i. To 'up arrow change 'space.'

To '0', '90' is changed.

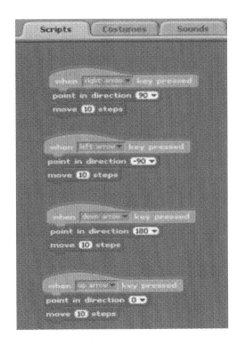

26. Now the Sprite is going to move in all four directions. It's time to test the program and move all across the screen, yourSprite.

27. As you like, rename the Sprite, e.g., Eater

28. Click "Save" to save the work and then name the file.

Chapter 7: Scratch 3.0 Introduction

A programming language block-based is Scratch used all over the world by millions of children for creating games, animation, and stories. The old version of Scratch that is 2.0, was Flash built, and by the year 2015, it was obvious that this Scratch requires a rewrite of JavaScript. A huge task was this, as having enormous libraries of code was the main thing.

So, a team at google (Blockly team) comes forward to do this task. A library is Blockly that makes things simpler for the coders or developers for adding block programming to the apps. On Blocky, many activities of web visual coding were made by 2015, through groups such as Makecode, App Inventor, Code.org. Nowadays, many developers use this Blocky code for teaching children about coding.

7.1 Scratch 3.0 Things to Know

Below is an overview of a few things regarding Scratch 3.0.

1. It has extra techniques for sharing and creating projects.

- On tablets, now you can remix, create, and share the projects besides desktop and computers.

- Many new sounds, backdrops, and characters are introduced in this.

- New sound editor and paint make it further easy for manipulating and remixing sound music and characters.

- Devices such as micro: bit and google translate like web services can be created by the extension system in it

2. Getting started new support in Scratch 3.0

- For the new user, new in editor learning is there.

- New videos bite-sized

- Updated Educator guides and Activity cards.

3. Overall, you will be in love with Scratch 3.0

- All previous accounts and projects will be working on this.

- All previous blocks for programming will be there with the new ones.

- Scratch previous offline versions (1.4 and 2.0) will be available also.

- It will be available and translated into different kinds of languages.

- IT IS FREE FOR EVERYONE.

7.2 SCRatch Advantages

Some main scratch programming advantages for kids are as follow:

- Becoming aware of modern technologies: becoming creator from consumer

- Increase the implementation of ideas and creativity

- Benefit and fun combination

- Essential skills development in cooperation and project management.

- Learning how to code in an enjoyable and simple way.

We are sure now that you have known about the benefits of coding or scratch benefits for the kid.

Chapter 8: Game on

In this chapter game on, you will study how to create a game with Scratch. Below are some blocks you will be using.

Input block

Input is a work that tells a computer what to do. By using input blocks, you can make code run when the player acts, like-- pressing a key or moving the mouse

Motion block

This motion block makes sprites move

Forever block

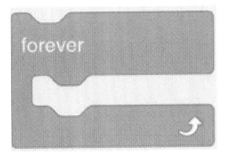

Next costume block

This block tells a fairy to choose different clothing, making it look unique. You can use this block to create simple cartoons.

Wait until block

By combining two blocks, you can make a code that runs when one fairy collides into another.

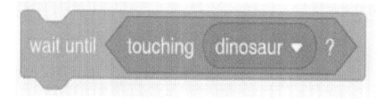

You will learn more when you start coding.

1. Fish in the sea

In this game, fish in the sea, you'll learn ways of controlling a sprite when it is moving around. You'll use a loop to help your sprite moving. Loop will help in the repetition of code. You can guide the fish by using pressing keys. If you want your game to look well, add a background.

1. Start Scratch

Open your default browser and search scratch.mit.edu. Click Create to get started.

2. No Cats

Cats aren't a good swimmer. If you want to delete your sprite, click on blue X.

3. Add a sprite

Click the **New Sprite** button

4. Select your Fish

Search pictures of fish in the sprite.

Click on the image of fish to choose your new Sprite

5. Add code

Move your code into the Coding Area

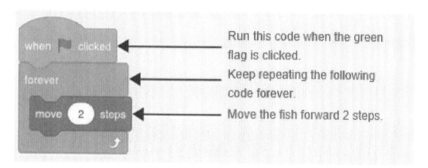

Click on the green flag to run your code. The fish should start moving forward slowly. It keeps moving until it reaches the Stage's edge because the move code block is inside the forever block.

6. Change direction

You can change the direction of the fish by using pressing keys. Move two more sections of code, shown here:

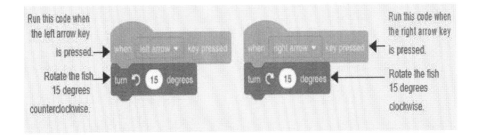

Run this code when the left arrow key is pressed.→ Rotate the fish 15 degrees counterclockwise.→

Run this code when the right arrow key is pressed. Rotate the fish 15 degrees clockwise.

Drag the fish to the left sideways of the Stage, then click on the green flag to run your code. Use can steer the fish using arrow keys.

7. **Add a background**

Click the new background icon

8. Select the underwater background

Roll through the backgrounds icon until you find underwater background

Click it to add the new background for your game.

In this game, you learned how to use a forever loop. A loop makes code in your game repeat over and over again.

2. Flap a Bat

It is a very popular game. Below are the steps for creating this game

In this game, the flying bat is controlled. The space button is used for giving an extra boost to the bird.

Sprites

Below sprites are needed for this game:

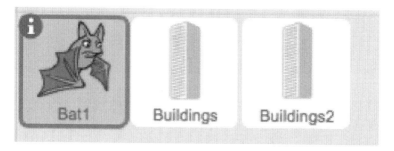

Flying the Bat

Bat is always falling downwards; the up / down movement is controlled by the axis Y. If we want something to occur, then the block of forever should be used.

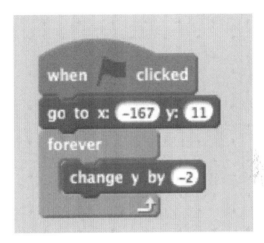

Try this to see that the bat falls slowly from above. By inserting in some costume change, the bat flying can be animated.

Giving an extra boost to the bat

Right now, the bat falls, and there is no method for keeping the bat flying. So, a space key is utilized for keeping the bat in the air. A negative no. is used for making the bat fall, and a positive no. is used for flying the bat.

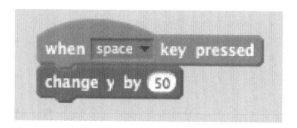

Moving the building

Across the screen, we want to move our building. Select the Sprite first of the building bottom.

The building is moved to the screen's right side all the way. It'll set the movement blocks X-Y, the correct position, which can be used.

Glide block can be used for setting the building position, which we like it moving towards.

To -240, X position is changed, and that is the least X no. of the game area.

When it's run, we can see the buildings' movement over the screen once only. So, it is needed to be changed to happen every time.

The issue next is the similar height buildings from the screen bottom. Somewhat randomness can be added to this.

As the screen bottom, half on the direction Y is 0 & -180, so due to this, negative numbers are used. The building's movement will be diagonal if it is tested. It is due to the glide block Y position setting. Y position needs to be a similar number that is randomly moved by us; if both the Y position and position of the glide block are the same at the starting and ending point, then it'll move straight.

The Y block is dragged in the glide block:

At the bottom, we've got a moving building across the screen.

Top Building

For the movement of Top building, the same technique is used, but positive numbers are used this time for random part. Make sure the building is placed in the beginning position.

The code should be like this

Hitting Buildings

A test is needed to know that the bat is hitting the building or not. Use an "if" block to test whether it is hitting the building. It must be checked whether the bat touches the building top or building bottom.

Bat sprite is selected, and the Script is modified by adding the "if" code.

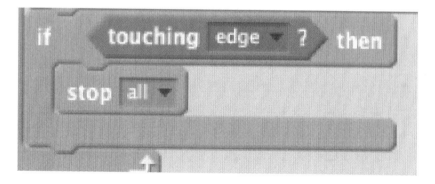

```
when   clicked
go to x: -167 y: 11
forever
    change y by -2
    next costume
    if    touching Buildings ▼ 7   or   touching Buildings2 ▼ 7   then
        go to x: -167 y: 5
        stop all ▼
```

Now, stop the game. It can be changed later on.

A test for checking the bat is hitting the game screen edge can also be added.

```
if    touching edge ▼ ?   then
    stop all ▼
```

Scoring

For making the game interesting, a scoring or point system must be introduced in this game. A score variable is used for scoring this game, and one building is selected for the reference of scoring. A Player gets one point as he crosses a building and reaches the endpoint

```
when [flag] clicked
set [Score ▼] to [0]
forever
    go to x: (248) y: (-134)
    change x by ( pick random (-10) to (-100) )
    glide (1) secs to x: (-248) y: ( y position )
    change [Score ▼] by (1)
```

To only a building, this needed to be done.

Increasing the level of difficulty

The game difficulty can be increased, and it will be more difficult for the player controlling the bat to pass the building as the player playing times increases. The game's speed can be increased, and the bat will move faster, and buildings will appear more quickly.

The speed variable is created for this purpose. Use this speed variable for reducing the time taken by it for the movement of building over the screen.

```
when  clicked
set  Score  to  0
set  Speed  to  6
forever
    go to x: 248 y: -63
    change y by  pick random -10 to -100
    glide  Speed  secs to x: -243 y:  y position
    change Score  by  1
    change Speed  by  0.5
```

The Sprite in which our scoring code was added that same building sprite is used. Glide added speed block would be needed by the other building.

```
when  clicked
forever
    go to x: 236 y: 216
    change y by  pick random 10 to 100
    glide  Speed  secs to x: -280 y:  y position
```

The game will get a bit faster than at some point speed will be very fast. It seems that the buildings are not moving. Another way is needed for setting the maximum game speed.

A test should be added to check if less than two secs is the speed, then change it back again to half a sec. Moreover, you can test different times to find the best result.

Extra

Give lives to the bat, and the lives are reduced each time the bat hits some building. More variables can be added that'll keep track of bat lives.

```
when [flag] clicked
set Lives to 5
go to x: -167 y: 11
forever
    change y by -2
    next costume
    if < touching Buildings ? > or < touching Buildings2 ? > then
        go to x: -167 y: 5
        change Lives by -1

    if < touching edge ? > then
        stop all
```

The game can end whenever the bat hits the building or edge,
but program it in such a way that life is decreased each time bat
hit some building. Make sure to move it to the screen middle for
giving another chance to the player.

There is also a need to see that all lives are utilized or not:

```
if < Lives = 0 > then
    stop all
```

3. Kiran and the magic crystals

This is another collecting game. Our brave astronaut Kiran has to travel around space, collecting the magic crystals. You'll use what you learned from the previous game and duplicate multiple sprites. You'll also use a new kind of loop and a special effect to make the magic crystals glow.

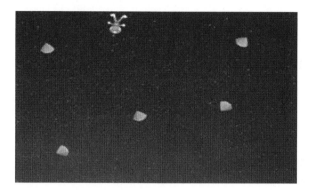

1. No cats in space

Space is bad for cats. Click the blue X to delete the cat.

2. Add a sprite

Click the New Sprite button

3. Choosing kiran

Scroll the sprites. Click Kiran to set them until you find Kiran.image for your new Sprite.

4. Add code to kiran

Make Kiran fly by dragging this code to the Coding Area:

Run the following code when the green color flag is clicked.

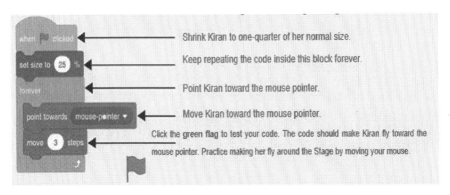

5. Add a sprite

Click the New Sprite button

6. Find the crystal

Scroll until you find the Crystal image.

Click it to select the image.

7. Code the crystal

To the Coding Area Drag this code to control the crystal:

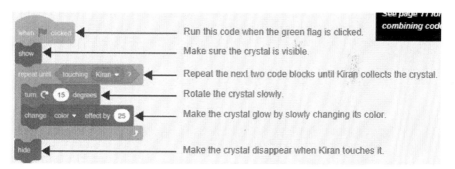

8. More crystals

In the sprites, first Right-click the Crystal sprite

Click Duplicate

Repeat step 8 until you've enough crystal spread out

9. We need stars

Click the new backdrop button

Scroll until you find the stars

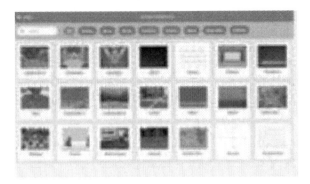

Test the code. For guiding Kiran around the Stage use the mouse pointer and collect the magic crystals.

In this game, when Kiran touch the crystals you made them disappear. You used a repeat until touching the loop to keep running some code until each crystal was found. This code created an animation that makes the game look more advanced and fun to play.

4. Cat on The Move

For our first game, Cat on the move, you'll learn how to move objects and change their direction. You'll use input blocks to let players interrelate with the computer by using the keyboard. Let's get started.

1. Start Scratch

To start using Scratch, open your default web browser, search scratch.mit.edu in the address bar, and then press the Enter key on the keyboard to search. Click the Create button on the main page when you are ready to start

2. Click events

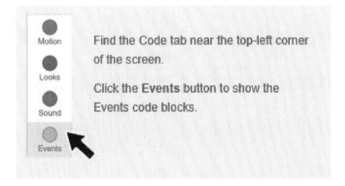

Find the Code tab near the top-left corner of the screen.

Click the **Events** button to show the Events code blocks.

You can drag the block into the coding area by pressing the mouse button.

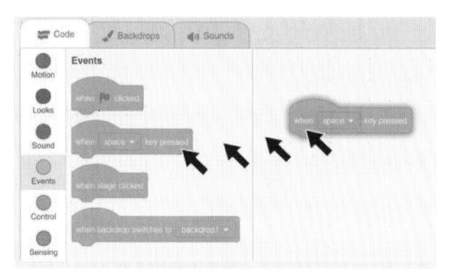

4. Set the key

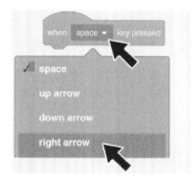

We make the sprite look like walking by switching different pictures. We call them frames in movies.

costume1   costume2

In Scratch, they're called costumes.

5. Get moving

Drag these code blocks into the Coding Area. You can find the blocks by using their colors.

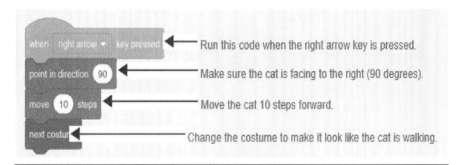

Run this code when the right arrow key is pressed.

Make sure the cat is facing to the right (90 degrees).

Move the cat 10 steps forward.

Change the costume to make it look like the cat is walking.

Click on the green flag to run your code. You can watch the cat movement after pressing the right arrow.

If you want to make the code run using the right arrow key, you have to go to the drop-down menu and select the right arrow key.

6. All directions

You have to add three more slices of code to let the Cat move in all direction:

Choose the key that will make each slice of the code run.

You have to change the direction of each segment. You can use the white arrow to select the direction to move in.

Now you can easily make a simple game that moves a sprite in a different direction.

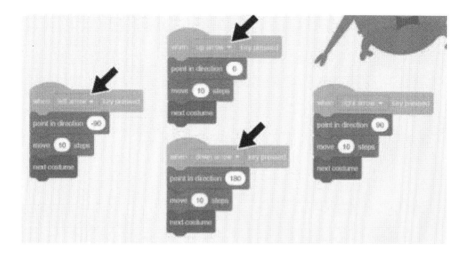

Click on the green flag to run your code. Move the Cat using arrow keys.

5. Cat and Mouse

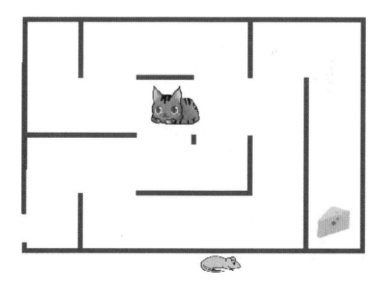

In this, you're a mouse who must get through some maze to eat the cheese. A cat will be there. Do not get caught by it. This program has a blank white background. Three sprites are there: a cat, the mouse, and cheese.

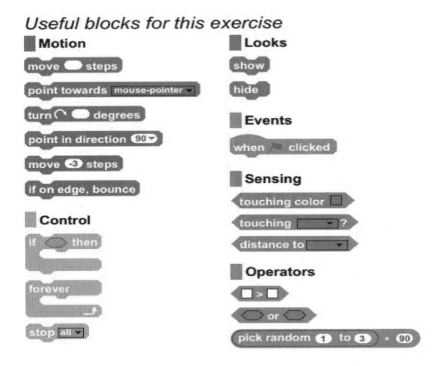

1. The Mouse

Firstly, write a program for making the mouse move. The mouse is controlled by the mouse pointer. This is done by turning the mouse towards the pointer and moving forward then.

2. Cheese

The mouse must eat cheese and by eating, we mean when it touches the cheese, the cheese disappears. For cheese sprite, the program is written. When the mouse touches or reaches towards cheese, the cheese disappears, and the cheese reappears when we touch the flag (green color).

3. The Cat

For the cat back and forth movement program is written. In a single direction, the cat should be moving. When the cat reaches the Stage's end, it starts moving in the opposite direction.

4. Caught

Make the program that If the mouse touches the cat, the game should end.

5. Walls

Maze must be added to make the game more exciting. To maze backdrop, modify the backdrop by clicking on the Stage. A problem is there that a mouse can cross the walls. So, for this use, collision detection. When the mouse moves or touches the walls, it should move back to the starting point as the walls are of blue color, so you just need to check if it's touching something blue. Before trying changes, make sure that the mouse is moved away from the walls.

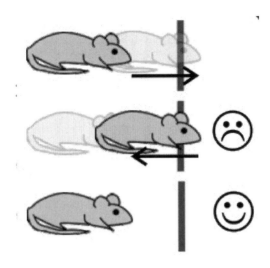

6. The Cat and Walls

Similarly, change the cat program when it touches the wall. It should move back to the starting point.

When the game is running, and the cat touches the wall, it should take a 180-degree turn and move back to the starting position.

7. Walking the Maze

The cat should be programmed smart enough to pass itself through the maze. You can go up, down, left, right, in the maze. If the cat touches some wall or moves to a corner, it should change the direction. Modify the program so that if the cat touches or bump into some wall, it changes its direction to 900,

1800, or 2700. By doing this, the cat will move by itself through the maze.

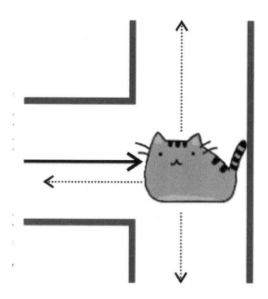

Make It: Less Jumpy

The mouse stats moving back & forth, when close to the mouse pointer, the mouse gets. It's because as it moves in the direction of the mouse pointer, it will go far and will end on the mouse pointer's other side.

6. Challenges

In this section, you will learn the basics of Scratch game making. For repeating code loops are used, and input blocks for responding to the mouse and keyboard. Moving and rotating the blocks let you move sprites around. You also used show, hide, next costume, and change color effect blocks to change how sprites look.

Challenge No. 1 DOG on The Move

Look at the previous code in the Cat on the Move game. Use a similar idea for making the program that moves the dog around the Stage. Start by removing the Cat sprite and changing it with a dog. Using the code in the Cat on the Move game, make the dog move by pressing the arrow keys.

Challenge No. 2 Animal Olympics

Cat and mouse depict how to make a game with the two moving sprites. For making a four-player game use a similar idea. Choose four to add while looking at the animal sprite. You can pick a different key for each animal sprite to move. Use the code on Cat and mouse to make every animal move when pressed some different key.

Challenge No. 3

Begin a new project in Scratch and choose a background. Remove the Cat sprite and put the Parrot in its place. Your Parrot should fly when you press the left and right arrow keys using what you learned in Fish in the Sea. Make the Parrot flutter its wings by using the next costume code block.

Challenge No. 4

In Bat in a Flap, you made a further complex game with different sprites. With a different background, start a new project. Add a dinosaur sprite instead of a bat for moving the dinosaur around use similar code to the bat sprite.

Challenge No. 5

It is similar to the Kiran and the Magic Crystals game. Create a new game where the Ripley sprite is flying around the Stage. Instead of crystals, add some aliens. Use the crystal code ideas to make the aliens change color and spin. Do some experiments to make new effects. When an alien Ripley reaches, it must disappear. Use code similar to that on the Kiran and the Magic Crystals game for making this game work.

Chapter 9: What's the Score?

1. Fruit picker

In the fruit picker game, a character Gobo is moved by using arrow keys. In the 1st round, you have to pick as many fruits as you can in the given time. The order of picking fruits is needed to be remembered in this game.

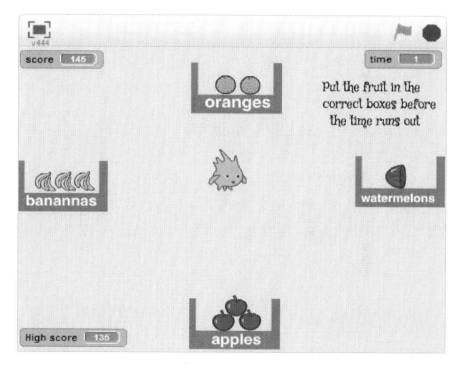

In the next round, the collected fruits are needed to be placed in the correct boxes, and you have to start from the fruits picked up in the last. For this round, there is a given time in which you have to put all the fruits. The game will be over if you put the fruits in a different box.

Step No. 1

1. A new project is created and named this Scratch project "Fruit Picker."

2. Gobo Sprite is added in place of Cat sprite. This Gobo sprite is present in the library.

3. Program it in such a way that Gobo sprite can move by using the arrow keys. A forever loop Is used with the sensing keypress for the movement of Gobo. This resulted in moving Gobo smoother than the When key pressed block.

2 Ways to make a sprite move with the arrow keys Which works best?

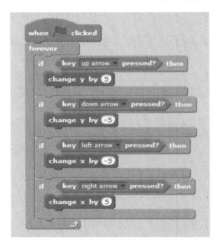 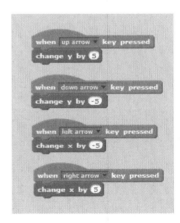

4. Four different costumes are used for creating a fruit sprite. These fruits' costumes are present in the library (bananas, apple, orange, watermelon). Only one Sprite is used, but it has four costumes.

5. Cloning is used for the appearance of multiple fruits on the screen **create clone of myself ▾**. The original Sprite is usually hidden that we're using for making the clones & then individual clones are shown in the event of when I start as the clone **when I start as a clone**. when cloning is done. Random no. s is used for positioning each clone in the screen area **pick random -140 to 140**. A random no. between 1 & 4 for picking to display which costume so that we've four kinds of randomly spread fruits on the screen as in the 1st picture above.

6. A type variable is created for clone using for storing the fruit type name represented by the clone. **Note:** when the type variable is created. The selection of this Sprite only is a must.

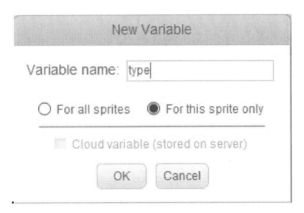

By selecting **"for this sprite."** Will let each clone to have a variable version of its own.

Use the nested block of if-else under the block of **when I start as the clone** for storing the fruit type in the variable of the type.

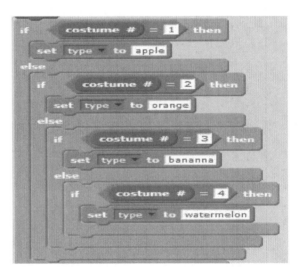

7. A list named **inventory** is created. For storing the list of the fruits, picked up by Gobo, this will be used.

8. A forever loop is added under the block of when I start as the clone. Inside this loop, test if Gobo touched the fruit. Hide it when it's touched, to the list of the inventory add the type of the fruit, play some sound effect, and then this clone is deleted.

9. A variable of the Score is added in such a way that whenever Gobo picks a fruit, the Score increases by 1. E.g., when you pick one fruit, you get one point. For the 2nd fruit, you'll get 2 points, and similarly, for the 3rd fruit, you'll get 3 points.

10. A variable of time is added, so when we click the green color flag, it starts off ten secs and then to 0 times down, and a message is broadcasted. For putting the code of the game, the best place is the Stage that that doesn't belong to a certain sprite.

Step No. 2

Now it's time to create the game second part-Gobo after fruit picking, has to put them in the boxes in the right order.

1. For every box, a sprite is added. Four box sprites will be needed, one for every fruit type. Every box sprite must have a different costume depicting different fruit amounts in the box. Empty start the box, and when the fruit is added by the Gobo to the next costume, the costume goes showing the fruit amount in the box.

2. To check the Gobo is touching box sprites, code is added. If it's touching, you require to check if inventory's last fruit item matches the box. If it is the oranges box, then you require to see if orange is the inventory's last fruit item. **Delete the last inventory** block is used for removing it. The next costume is used for adding to the box. Also, a sound is played, and the Score is increased. If the inventory's last fruit item isn't matching, then the game will be over- a message of the' game over' should broadcast.

3. Forever loop inside checking will be done, so while you're in touch with the box after checking the last inventory item, immediately it will check the item that is next without providing the chance for moving away, and the game will end at once. A forever loop pause is needed after one check till the Gobo moves away.

4. The time variable is set to have 20 secs for putting the fruit inside the boxes. After that game will be over.

5. A stage backdrop is created that can produce a sound & a graphic is displayed that showing game over when the game gets over.

6. Make a variable of high Score that will update if greater is the Score than the high Score.

---

2. Brick breaker game

A very famous game is this in which the player has to control the screen bottom paddle. This paddle is for bouncing the ball, which is breaking the blocks at the screen top, as shown in the image below. The games end when the ball passes the bottom battle. This game programming is simple, but it can seem boring. We are now going to guide you in making this game more interesting and colorful by adding further effects and animation.

An iterative process will be used: firstly, the basic game will be made, and after that, a few improvements will be added. This will result in a further professional looking game. The below figures depict the before and after brick game after polishing or adding new features to it.

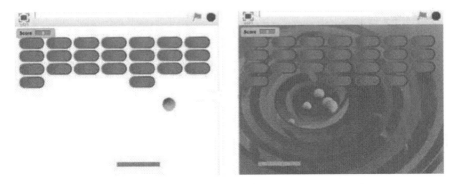

Design sketching

First of all, we start with the game, drawing how it should be. The sketch or design for this game might seems similar to the below figure.

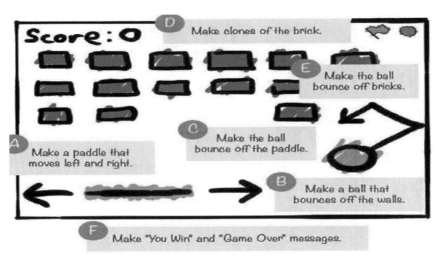

Left and the right moving paddle is made

The paddle will be controlled by the mouse. The ball gets bounced after hitting the paddle, and if the ball does not hit the paddle and gets past then, the player will lose.

Paddle Sprite Creation

There is no need to change the cat for this game. So, click the mouse right button on the first Sprite1 in the list of Sprite and delete is selected. Now the Sprite is painted by clicking on the new sprite paint button present next to the new Sprite. Use the rectangle tool now for drawing the wide rectangle after the appearance of the Paint Editor.

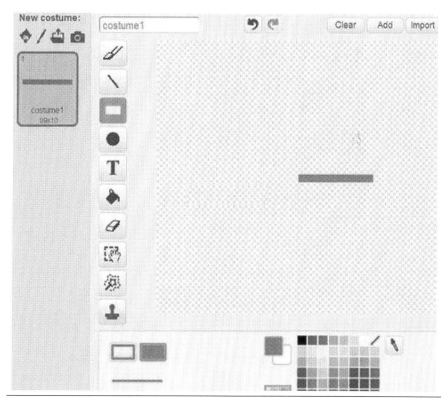

We have made a Green color paddle, but one can choose the color as he/she likes. It will be more difficult to bounce the ball if the paddle Is short. You can also make paddles of different sizes for making an easy or hard game. Info Area is opened by clicking on the button, and now Sprite is renamed.

Now for programming the paddle sprite, code is added, and this is done so that the bottom paddle moves along the stage bottom with the movement of the mouse.

```
when 🏳 clicked
set rotation style don't rotate ▼
go to x: 130 y: -140
forever
    point towards mouse-pointer ▼
    move 10 steps
    set y to -140
```

Constantly moves the paddle sprite towards the mouse ten steps directly but set the y position to -140.

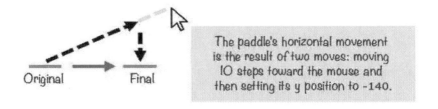

Original   Final

The paddle's horizontal movement is the result of two moves: moving 10 steps toward the mouse and then setting its y position to -140.

By setting y position to -140 only to the right and left will move the Paddle sprite.

Rotation styles exploration

When the sprite direction is changed by setting the rotation style, then how will the Sprite look? The three styles of rotation are left-right all around and do not rotate.

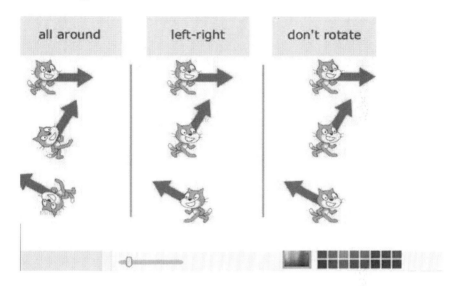

When to all around, we set the Sprite, it'll exactly face in the direction points. This would not work for in the side view game such as basketball game due to sprite upside down when left faces its direction. In games like these, the rotation style of left-right will be used. Only 90° right side or -90° left side the Sprite will face whatever is near to the direction of Sprite. Moreover, if you do not want to rotate the Sprite even when the direction changes, the rotation style is set to do not rotate.

As we are changing the direction of Paddle sprite, there is also a need to set the rotation style of Sprite with the block of **set rotation style.** The programming of paddle sprite is that its face and move to the mouse, yet we like the Sprite to look horizontal and flat always, to do not rotate set the rotation style.

Saving point

The green color flag is clicked now for checking the so far code. Test the paddle sprite is following the mouse by moving it, and the paddle is at the stage bottom. Then ifs everything is fine, save the program by clicking on the red color stop sign.

In the Sprite library, there are many sprites that we can use for making the ball, but it's best to use the Sprite of the tennis ball for games like these.

2. Creating the Sprite of Tennis ball

The Sprite of a tennis ball is selected from the library window of Sprite by clicking on the button beside New Sprite; **choose Sprite from the library.**

At (0,0) position in the stage center, starts the Sprite of the tennis ball as the game start. After that, down points the Sprite of the tennis ball and right to the Sprite of the paddle. Next, the Sprite of Tennis ball begins to move in a **forever loop**. When at the stage edge touch the Sprite of the tennis ball, in some new direction, it will bounce.

Saving Point

For checking the so far code, the green color is selected. Check the around the movement of the Sprite of the tennis ball, and the edges bounce. Note that the paddle tennis ball won't bounce off as the code for this is not added yet. To save the program, click on the red color stop sign.

B. Paddle bouncing ball Creation

Till now, code for this is not added, so for this program now, you should add code. So, the ball bounces after striking the walls.

3. Adding Bounce code to the tennis ball sprite

To the Sprite of Tennis ball, add the below code so that it bounces after hitting the Sprite of Paddle. For this, a new broadcast message is needed to be created to bounce.

In Script no. 1, you will use the broadcasting message for controlling what will happen in Script no. 2 when the paddle is hit by the ball.

The 180-degree point in direction code in Script no. 2 might appears to be some mysterious, yet this equation will calculate the ball bouncing direction on the basis of the current direction of the ball. If at 45 degrees (up & right) is pointed to the ball, then when the ball bounces the brick bottom, the new direction of the ball will be 135 degrees (down & right) as 180-45 is equal to 135. If up & left is pointed the ball (-45°), then as it gets to bounce off the brick bottom, the new direction would be (225°) down and left as 180(-45) is equal to 225.

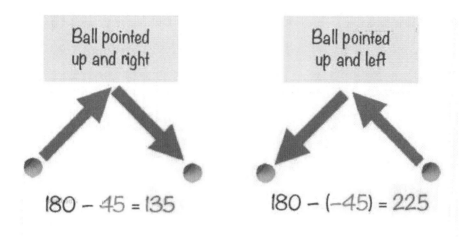

A broadcast message will be used again in the program later when the code for making the ball bounce after hitting the Brick is added.

Saving point

To test the so far made code, click on the green color flag. Be sure that after hitting the paddle, bounce off the tennis ball. Save the program after clicking the red color stop sign.

Cloning Exploration

The block of **create clone of myself** makes the sprites duplicate; that's called a clone. Very handy is this feature whenever multiple copies of some object are required to be made in the game, like cloning many same looking bad guys, for a player some collecting coins, or the bricks you want to hit in the game of Brick Breaker.

Let's have a look at the working of clones. In a new tab, open the Scratch, then a new program is created. Now to the Sprite of a cat, this code is added.

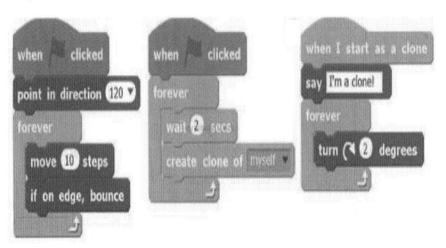

Script no. 1 results in bouncing the cat sprite around the Stage, like the Sprite of a tennis ball that does in the game of Brick Breaker. But in Script no. 2, a clone is created again & again, after every two secs. Script no. 3 uses the block of when I start like clone for controlling the cloned sprite behavior. Now run this code and see what will happen.

The real Sprite of Cat, around the Stage, bounce off. Every two secs a sprite duplicate is created(clones). Every clone then begins to turn due to Script no. 2.

D Making Brick clones

Many bricks are needed now in this game, so for this, a sprite of Brick is created, and then it's cloned using the block of **create clone**.

4. Brick Sprite Addition

Next to the New sprite button, **Choose Sprite from the library** is clicked. And the button two sprite is selected from the window of Sprite Library. Info area is opened by clicking on the button i, and this Sprite is renamed Brick.

Now by selecting the category of orange data, there is a need to make a new variable and. Click on the button of **Make a variable.** This variable Score is named, then to **for all sprites**, set it. The below code is added to the Sprite of the Brick.

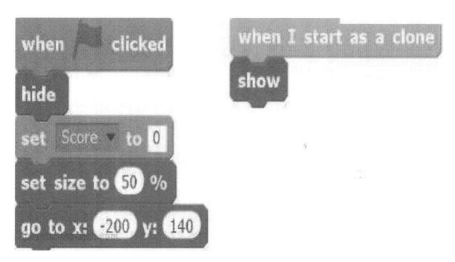

To 0, set the variable of the Score, at the game beginning to reset previous game any points.

The block of the **hide** itself hides the original Sprite by 50 % shrink in size, and to the Stage top-left corner it moves (-200,140).

5. Brick Sprite Cloning

Many Brick rows are required from this game of Brick Breaker. For making bricks rows, the original Sprite we will move across the screen top, creating clones trail. Add the below code to the Sprite of the Brick. Don't confuse the blocks of **set x to** & **change by x.**

```
when [flag] clicked
hide
set Score to 0
set size to 50 %
go to x: -200 y: 140
repeat 4
    repeat 7
        create clone of myself
        change x by 65
    set x to -200
    change y by -30
```

Brick sprite clones are created by this code in the game for all the bricks, as shown.

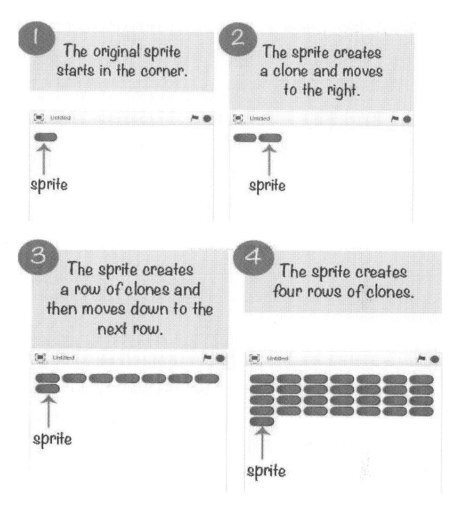

1. The original sprite starts in the corner.

2. The sprite creates a clone and moves to the right.

3. The sprite creates a row of clones and then moves down to the next row.

4. The sprite creates four rows of clones.

To the stage corner (top-left) at -200, 140, moves the original Sprite. Then the block of repeat 7 moves repeatedly right 65 steps while making itself clones for creating 7 Brick clones' rows. The block of repeat 4 repeats the code of row creation for creating Brick clones four-row. 7 brick clones X 4 rows results in twenty-eight Brick clones. In the previous fig, the 29th Brick is the real Sprite, not the clone, & we will hide it next.

The real Sprite itself hides after the creation of all clones. Now clones are all the bricks on the Stage, so there is no need in code duplicating under the block of when I start like clone for the real Sprite.

Imagine Sprite duplicating in place of cloning. Then if you want to modify the code, then you would have to modify all twenty-eight Brick sprites. A lot of time is saved by cloning.

E. Ball Bouncing of Bricks Making

The Sprite of the tennis ball bounces off the paddle sprite and the stage edges. Let's make now the ball bouncing off bricks.

6.Brick Sprite Bounce Code Adding

Match as the below Brick sprite code

When the Brick sprite strikes the Sprite of a tennis ball, the bounce message is broadcasted by the Sprite of Brick, which brings into play the code of Tennis ball; the direction of the ball changes when it strikes the paddle. 1 is added to the Score of the player by the program, and code eliminates itself.

Saving Point

To test the so far made code, click on the green color flag. Make sure the stage top part is brick clones filled and disappears the clones when the Sprite of Tennis ball bounces after hitting. To save the program, click on the red color stop sign.

"Game Over" and "You win" Messages making

Two further sprites are needed for this game, but they will not appear till the game is over. You can create these with the text tool of the 'Paint Editor.' If all the clones of the Brick are broken by the player, then the Sprite of 'You Win' will be displayed by the program. If the tennis ball passes the paddle, then the Sprite of 'Game Over' will be displayed by the program.

7. Modifying the Code Tennis Ball Sprite

When the Sprite of tennis ball crosses the Sprite of Paddle, that's when the Y position of Sprite of the tennis ball is lower than -140; the game is over now. As the game gets over or end, the Sprite of the tennis ball must broadcast a message of the game over. To the Sprite of the tennis ball, add the below code.

For this, you need to create the broadcast message of the game over.

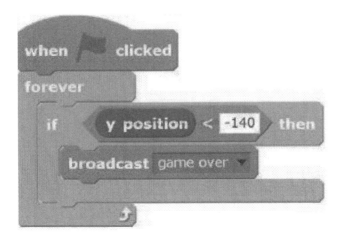

Let's make the next Sprite. The broadcast of the game over will tell the Sprite of the game over to appear.

Game Over Sprite Creation

Besides the button of New Sprite, click on the button of **Paint new sprite**. Write in red **game Over** by using the test tool after the appearance of Paint Editor.

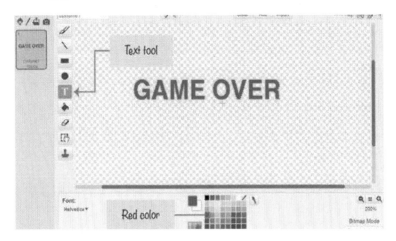

Info area is opened after clicking on the | button, and now the Sprite can be renamed to the game over. Add the below code to the Sprite of Game over.

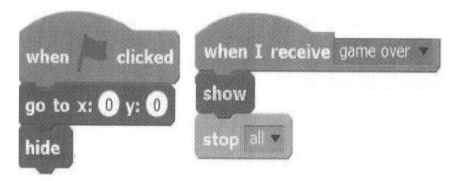

Until receiving the broadcast of the game over, remain hidden the Sprite. Block of Stop all the stops the sprites (all of them) from moving.

Saving Point

To test the so far code, click on the green color flag. Allow the ball to get past the paddle to make sure the appearance of the Sprite of the game over and stops the program. Save the program

9. You Win Sprite Creation

Besides the New sprite button, click the button of Paint new sprite. Write, you win In any color, you like (we have chosen green color) by using the text tool in the paint editor.

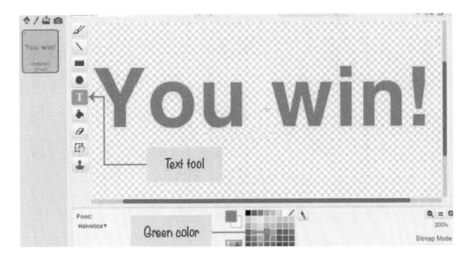

Text tool

Font: Helvetica

Green color

Bitmap Mode

Info area is opened after clicking on the ⅰ button, and now the Sprite can be renamed you win. Add the following code to this Sprite.

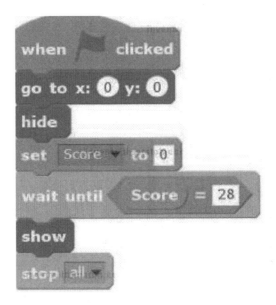

As with the Sprite of the game over, the Sprite of you win is hidden till the condition is reached. All 28 bricks must be broken down in this game by the player, so the score=28 condition is met. The Sprite you win will be displayed, and all different Sprite will be stopped from moving by the program with **stop all**.

Saving Point

To test the so far code, click on the green color flag. Make sure the appearance of you wins Sprite, and the program is topped after all bricks breaking. For making a faster winning game, temporarily modify block 28, wait until Score to 1, wait until Score. Then only one Brick is needed to be broken. Save the program.

The entire program

Below is the full code for the complete program. You can check the code you made with this one if some program you made is not working.

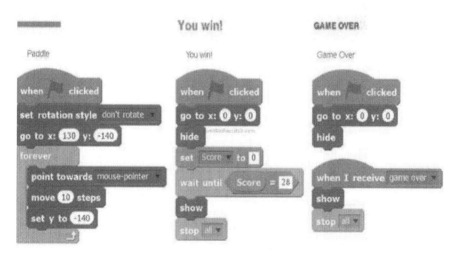

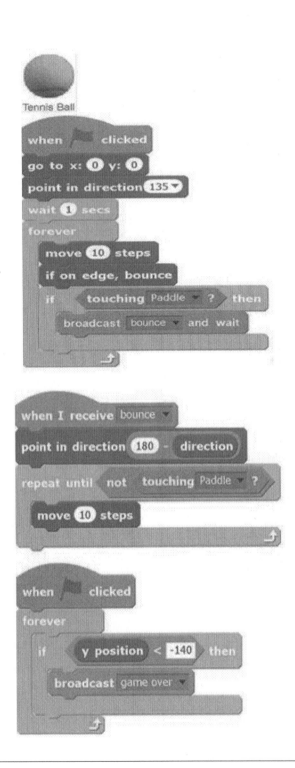

Tennis Ball

when 🚩 clicked
go to x: 0 y: 0
point in direction 135 ▼
wait 1 secs
forever
    move 10 steps
    if on edge, bounce
    if touching Paddle ▼ ? then
        broadcast bounce ▼ and wait

when I receive bounce ▼
point in direction 180 - direction
repeat until not touching Paddle ▼ ?
    move 10 steps

when 🚩 clicked
forever
    if y position < -140 then
        broadcast game over ▼

Brick

```
when [flag] clicked
hide
set Score to 0
set size to 50 %
go to x: -200 y: 140
repeat 4
    repeat 7
        create clone of myself
        change x by 65
    set x to -200
    change y by -30
```

```
when I start as a clone
show
forever
    if touching Tennis Ball ? then
        broadcast bounce
        change Score by 1
        delete this clone
```

3. Challenges

1. Challenge No.1 Pong

In this project, you have to create a game. This game includes interactions between sprites, scores, and levels. It is similar to the game of pong, where the goal is to keep the Sprite from getting past you.

Need to do

Create two sprites: a paddle for the user to control and a ball the user will be playing with.

Sprite interactive, make your paddle.

Bring to life your game.

Moreover,

How to add difficulty to the game? The creation of different levels use a timer or scorekeeping are some examples you can do.

Experiment with changing the look of your game by editing the backdrops.

Explore using different keypresses to control your sprites

Challenge No.2 Bowling

The player knocks pins by bowling a ball in this game. The space button should be used to fire the ball, and the arrow keys control its movement. Record the Score.

Hint

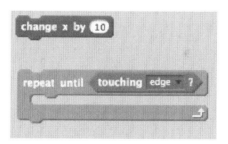

Challenge No.3: 9 - Magic 8 Ball

Make a magic eight ball or an all-knowing cat so that it gives you some random answer when you click it.

Hint

A list can be used for storing the options for magic 8 ball.

Challenge No.4 - Coins Collection Game

Collect the coins by moving the cat with the arrow keys.

Part 1: With arrow keys, control the cat.

Part 2: **Hide the coin when the cat touches it.**

Further Challenge: See if you can keep track of the player's coins in a variable.

Chapter 10: Math matters

1. Snake

Snake game is a very famous game that is still played by many kids and adults on their cell phones and computer. This game is also known as Worm or Nibbles. In this game, arrow buttons are used to move the snake. Apples are there in the game, and when the snake touches those apples, it gets longer, and its length increases, but the area remains the same. When the snake crashes with its own body or stage edges, the game ends, so you have to avoid the snake crashing with its own Body or the edges as it becomes more difficult when the length of the snake increases. The snake movement cannot be slowed down.

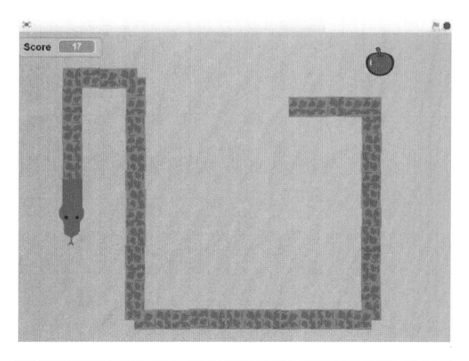

You've to measure the snake length in inches when it gets longer as the snake does not have feet.

Design sketching

Firstly, sketch the game.

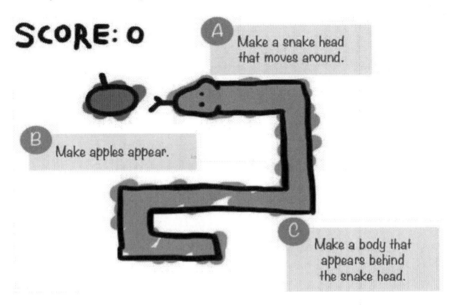

Make A controllable Snake head

A controllable snake head Is made, which can be controlled by the player by using the keyboard's arrows. Always the head will move in the forward direction. Arrows will only change its direction. A snake body will be created later on.

1. Head Sprite Creation

The background can be made more interesting. In the list of Sprite, click the Stage, then the backdrop tab is clicked. Now upload the file. And upload any downloaded file you like.

Next to the new Sprite, click on the new sprite paint button for drawing the snake head. Draw a snake head view top-down, which faces right in the editor(paint). As the scratch sprites face 900 (right side), the head is drawn facing right. Rename the head sprite after creating it.

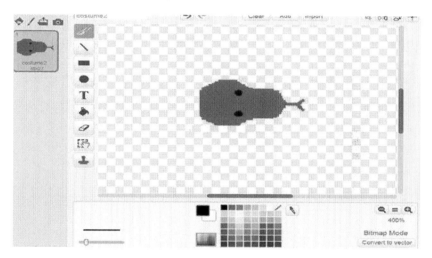

At the scratch editor top, use the grow tool or shrink tool for growing or shrinking head sprite.

To head Sprite, add the following code

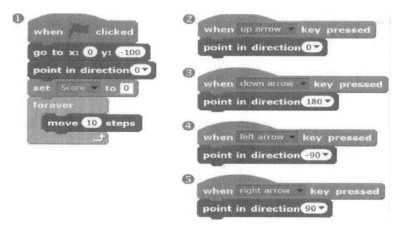

The starting direction and starting point are set by script 1(straight up or 0 degrees) for the snake's head. It will set the player to 0 Score, and for this, a variable for all Sprite named "Score" is required. A variable can be created by clicking on the button of Making variable in the category orange data. A snake has to move all the time, so 10 steps forever move loop is required in the program.

2,3,4 and 5 scripts are the short scripts that'll handle the controls. Directions are corresponding to the down arrow, up arrow, right arrow, & left arrow keys.

Saving Point

For testing the code made so far, click on the flag (green). Arrow keys are tested (snake head is correctly directed by these left, right, up, and down arrow keys). If the code is working fine, press the sign of red stop to save the program you have made up till now.

Explore: if the key pressed versus when key pressed

In this program, the code block of when key pressed to move the player and its used when once the key Is likely to be clicked.

In the game of maze, the block of if-then within the forever loop moves the player, and if the key pressed is used when some key is to be pressed & held down.

In this Snake program, the code of the block when key pressed proceed the player, and it's used when some key is supposed to be clicked once.

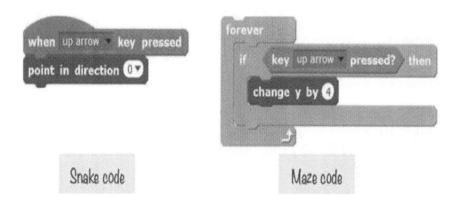

Snake code   Maze code

In these programming ways, the controls of players aren't the same. Make sure the correct code blocks are used for the project you're creating. As always on the move is the snake, and when the players press the key, the snake changes its direction. So, this is the reason for using the block of when key pressed in the snake game.

2. Apple

After completing the snake movement, now it's time to make the apple appear, which will snake eat to get longer.

Apple Sprite

Choose the sprite button; besides the button of New Sprite, it is present. Then apple sprite is selected from the library. Add the following code:

```
when [flag] clicked
set size to 50 %
forever
    if < touching Head ▼ ? > then
        change Score ▼ by 1
        go to x: ( pick random -220 to 220 ) y: ( pick random -160 to 160 )
```

The above code will make the apple disappear as it is eaten by the snake, and then appears the apple in some different places. From random no. s, a new position is selected, like rolling a dice. The Score is also added by the Script every time the snake eats the apple.

Saving point

Again test the code by clicking the green color flag and test the game now whether it's working fine (apple move to a different location when snake' head come in contact with the apple, and the Score also increases by 1 point). If it's fine, then save it by clicking the sign of red stop.

Snake body creation

Now it's time to create the snake body, which will increase in its length as it eats/touches the apple.

3. Body Sprite creation

For creating a new Sprite paint, the sprite button is pressed. Using a similar snake head color draw a square. By pressing the center button of Set costume and then the square middle, make sure that in the square middle, the costume center is.

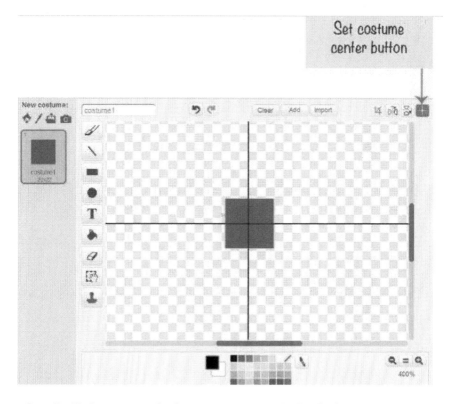

The " i" button of the Sprite is clicked for opening the information area. Now Sprite's Body is renamed.

4. Creating the 2nd costume of body sprite

Right-click costume 1 in the editor (paint) and duplicate is selected. Change the square color to some different color, e.g., light green color using the fill tool. This program has used a light green color for the snake body and dark green color for the snake head. It's for checking the snake crashing. Different patterns can also be added to this color top.

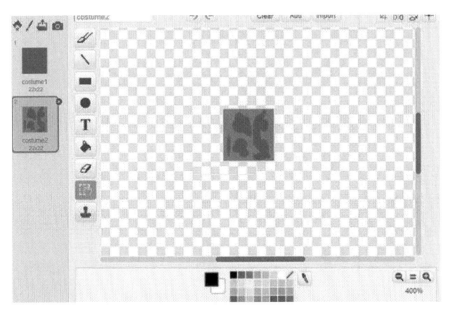

Anything can be drawn on the snake's body as you are the maker of this game like some clothes: feather boa, a boa tie, etc. or simply leave it without clothes. If using clothes, make sure to have the color difference between costumes 2 and 1 and square shape are the body costumes.

5. Body sprite coding

To body sprite, the below code is added by clicking the script tab. We design the code so that Sprite of the Body always follows the Sprite of the head & generates its own clones.

```
when    clicked                    when I start as a clone

switch costume to costume1 ▼      point in direction  pick random 0 to 3 * 90

forever                           wait 0.1 secs

   go to Head ▼                   switch costume to costume2 ▼

   wait 0.01 secs                 wait  Score / 5 secs

   create clone of myself ▼       delete this clone
```

Under the script 1 block, when flag (green) clicked, the code of the original body sprite runs. As all over the Stage, head sprite moves, trails of clones of Body are created by its path body sprite.

The code of clones of Body runs under script 2. In an arbitrary direction, body clone points when it is first made. The clone (Body) faces 0 or 90 or 180, or 2700 due to the block 0 to 3 * 90. due to this rotation, slightly different looks the body segment.

From the Stage, clones need to be deleted eventually, so the snake's length does not keep on growing. So, for some time, every clone waits on the basis of the variable of Score in the block wait score per 5 secs before itself deleting. This much time each clone waits, so deleted body clones are the clones (Body) made first.

The variable of Score is increased by eating apples. The clone (Body) waiting time before itself deleting increases as there is an increase in the Score variable. The snake looks longer due to this longer waits as on Stage; further clones of Body remain. So, the snake gets longer more by eating more apples.

0.5 secs or 0 sec is the wait when to 0 the Score is set. 1/5 secs or .2 secs is the wait when to 1 the Score is set. 2/5 sec or .4 secs is the wait when to 2 the Score is set. Wait time of further .2 secs is added by each point, and this results in a longer snake. Similarly, the game difficulty increases as the length of the snake increases.

Saving point

The code is tested on this point by clicking on the green color flag. See if the Body of the snake or its length increases after eating apples. Save the program if it's ok by clicking the sign of red stop.

6. Snake crashing detection in the wall or itself

Run the code (game over) when I receive when with the edges or with itself the snake crashes. For 2 secs, Ouch will be displayed by the Head sprite, and then the game ends. For all the crashes, just the code is put rather than writing this code twice under the block (game over) when I receive, so game over is broadcasted at every crash. You can modify the code in the same block script if you like to modify it.

To Head sprite, add the below code:

```
when         clicked
go to x: 0 y: -100
point in direction 0
set Score to 0
forever
    move 10 steps
    if    touching color    ?    then
        broadcast game over    and wait
    if    touching edge    ?    then
        broadcast game over    and wait
```

```
when I receive game over
say Ouch! for 2 secs
stop all
```

Block of Touching color: the first test of if loop if the snake crashes into itself. The color used in this block for this situation must be the same as costume 2. The vertical and horizontal boundaries are tested by the next if statements. The broadcast of the game over is sent whenever the snake crosses them. It depends on the player quick and smart enough to prevent crashing.

The Sprite code of the Body is below again:

```
when     clicked
switch costume to costume1
forever
    go to Head
    wait 0.01 secs   ←——— Added a slight pause
    create clone of myself
```

Body Sprite of the 2nd costume has the light color that is used by Head sprite for detecting itself snake crashing. Due to Body clones' creation at the exact location as Head sprite, they're in touch with the head. This is the reason for pausing the detection of the crash during the creation of the clone. In the absence of this wait, Head sprite is going to think that it has crashed in the just created Body clone as it's touching light color.

Saving point

The code is tested by clicking the green color flag. Now check the crashing of the snake by crashing the snake into itself or the wall. If there is a problem like a snake is crashing and not touching the edges or walls, then increase 0.1, 0.2, or even more wait time. Or when the snake is not crashing into something. If everything is fine, save the program by clicking the sign of red stop.

The Full program

Below is the image of the full program. If there is any problem with your program or it's not working, you can compare your program with this code.

Head

```
when [flag] clicked
go to x: (0) y: (-100)
point in direction (0 ▼)
set [Score ▼] to [0]
forever
    move (10) steps
    if < touching color [ ] ? > then
        broadcast [game over ▼] and wait
    if < touching [edge ▼] ? > then
        broadcast [game over ▼] and wait
```

```
when I receive [game over ▼]
say [Ouch!] for (2) secs
stop [all ▼]
```

```
when [up arrow ▼] key pressed
point in direction (0 ▼)
```

```
when [down arrow ▼] key pressed
point in direction (180 ▼)
```

```
when [left arrow ▼] key pressed
point in direction (-90 ▼)
```

```
when [right arrow ▼] key pressed
point in direction (90 ▼)
```

Apple

```
when [flag] clicked
set size to (50) %
forever
    if < touching [Head ▼] ? > then
        change [Score ▼] by (1)
        go to x: (pick random (-220) to (220)) y: (pick random (-160) to (160))
```

Body

when ⚑ clicked
switch costume to costume1
forever
  go to Head
  wait 0.01 secs
  create clone of myself

when I start as a clone
point in direction (pick random 0 to 3) * 90
wait 0.1 secs
switch costume to costume2
wait (Score / 5) secs
delete this clone

2. Space Battle

Step No. 1 Stage Setting

As in this game, the battle will occur in space, so an outer space like backdrop is needed. Go to the library for selecting stars backdrop.

Step No. 2: Sprites Bringing

Three sprites are needed in this game (space monsters, enemy, and the Rocketship). Special bullets for killing monsters are also needed. Click the sprite button for choosing the three Sprites. Add 3 sprites by going to the library one at each time.

Step No. 3: Rocketship Preparation

Make sure to select the Sprite of Rocketship.

1. Evive is connected to the computer, and PictoBlox is opened. Then as the board, it is chosen, and the menu of connect appropriate port is selected. Remember uploading the firmware.

2. In the area of scripting, the block of when flag click is dragged and dropped.

3. The block of go to x () y () is dragged and dropped below the block of when flag click. As 0 set x and as -140 set y. This is going to be the position of the Rocketship initially.

4. Rocket size is adjusted by using the block of set size to () %. Change it to forty percent of the real size.

5. At the start of the game, add the music this time. The start sound () is added from the palette of Sound. Now press on the tab of Sound. In the palette block, beside the tab of code, it is present. In the left bottom corner, there is a button for choosing Sound. From the library, video game one is selected.

6. On the tab of code, click for going back to the Scriptwriting. From the block of start sound () down drop, the Video Game one is selected.

7. Two variables creation is needed now. One for monitoring Rocketship health & the other for keeping track of monsters killed by us. Create the Score and Health variable by going to the palette of the variable.

8. The initial Health value is set to three, and the Score is set to 0.

9. A block of forever is dragged and dropped.

The entire Script is below:

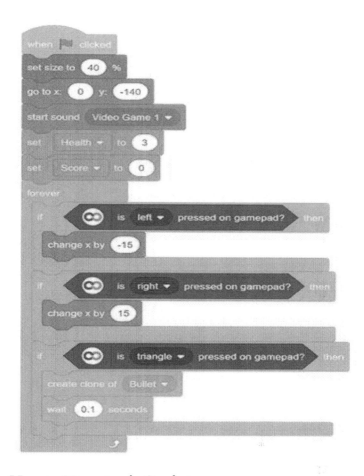

Step No. 4: Monster's Scripts

Two scripts will be written: one for the creation of several monsters and the other for action assigning to the monsters

Make sure to select the Sprite of the monster.

Multiple Monsters Creation

1. The block of when flag click is dragged and dropped.

2. The block of forever is dragged and dropped.

3. Inside it, the block next costume is dragged and dropped; then, a clone is created.

4. The block of wait () secs is added, and time is set as 2 secs.

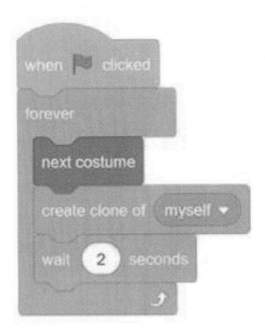

Monsters Action Assigning

Randomly the monster should come from the stage top and move downward gradually until either at the stage bottom they reach or are shot down by you. If you hit them with the bullet, the Score must increase by 1, and they must disappear: however, if our Rocketship is touched by any monster, it will harm you. So, the variable of health value is reduced by 1. If the value reaches 0, it will result in the ending of the game. On the basis of this logic, the Script is below.

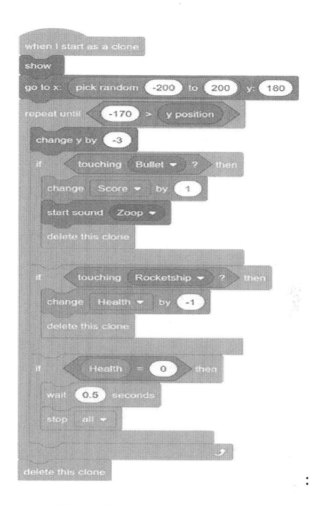

Step No. 5: Bullets Shooting

Make sure to select the Sprite of the bullet.

1. The block of when I start as the clone is dragged and dropped.

2. The size is set, and the laser 2 sound is added.

3. To the exact Rocketship initial position, go, so it looks that the bullets are fired by the ship.

4. The block of repeat is dragged and dropped for deciding the bullet movement duration. Upward it must move until it reaches the stage top or hit some monster. Y coordinate of it must be changed every time 12 steps for providing upward movement.

The Script is Below.

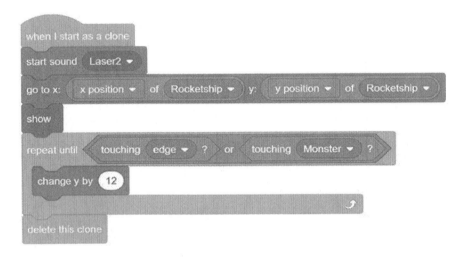

Play the game.

Step No. 7: Conclusion

After this, you are all ready to play this game and protect the universe by killing those monsters. Best of luck.

3. Jumping with Scratch

Step No. 1

Different platforms and characters are made. Platforms of the same colors must be created.

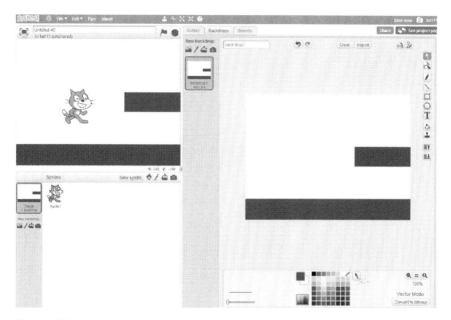

Step No. 2

For jump, a space bar button is used.

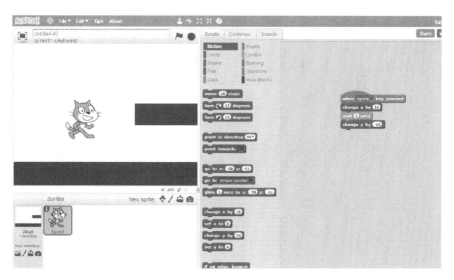

Step No. 3

For Y Velocity, Create a variable (the falling speed)

Step No. 4

Gravity is Introduced so that the character falls

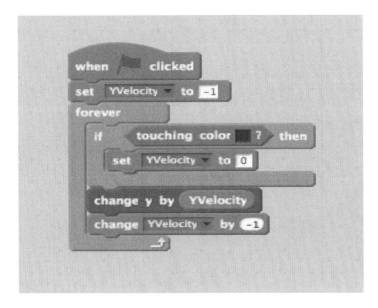

Step No. 5

Using Y Velocity to re-code the jump so that smoothly the cat jumps.

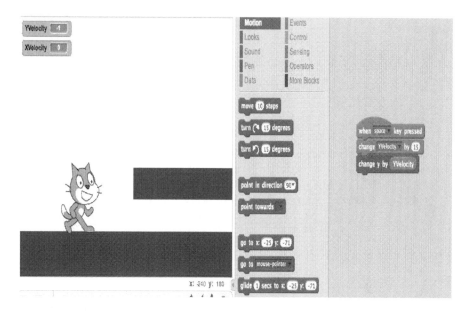

Step No. 6

Acceleration and velocity are introduced so that the character does not fall at a similar speed

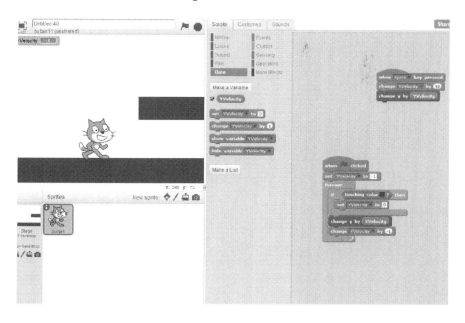

Step No. 7

An x velocity variable is added to slide the character.

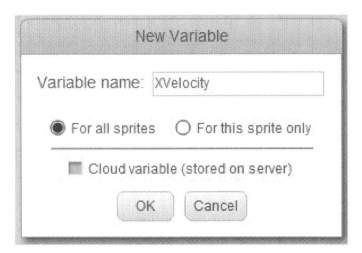

Step No. 8

Using X Velocity, Make the cat slide around

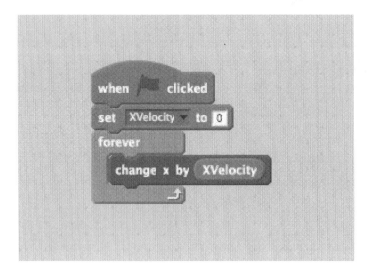

Step No. 9

Our velocity is Changed when pressed the right & left arrows.

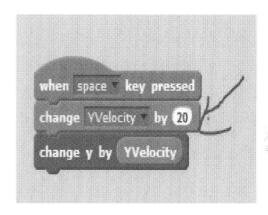

Step No. 10

The Y Velocity is changed for higher jumping

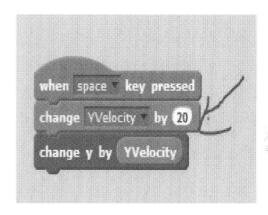

---

4. Tower builder

Tower Defense Game

In this game, there is a tower that aims at enemies and kills them. Making these kinds of games is a bit hard as tower building, aiming and cloning are required in these sorts of games.

After the introduction of the cloning feature in Scratch, this tower defense game becomes quite popular. For this game, cloning is required as the same tower, target, and projectile are allowed by cloning. Below is the full step to step guide for making this wonderful game from Scratch. Assume the following from this tutorial:

- There are towers in this game firing at enemies

- Front enemies are always attacked by these towers.

Game Planning

Getting all things ready like artwork, etc. before final programming is very helpful, and due to this, we know the exact visualization that how this game will work. E.g., the movement of enemies along some proper path needs to be done, and this can't be done without the map creation and the visualized path. Different factors, like the menu, should also be considered.

Main Menu creation

If you want the main menu that simply a button will be enough. Below is an example.

This type of button can be made in the paint editor of Scratch easily. Besides this button, the menu has some background typically. An image made in the Stage can be the background.

Programming

The below Script is added to the button simply for programming the main menu:

Structure of Enemies

Enemies need to have different costumes as these enemies would have many layers to break down. We can use an enemy Sprite for all the enemies that'll be in the game because of cloning enemies' costumes will be organized in the Costume pane, so a sequential layer order will be there. This would assist in the transition properly in the project scripting.

Beginning Rounds

The round must not begin immediately as the game starts. A start button is there typically in which before clicking, one has the time for assembling towers. Below, Script can be inserted into the start button.

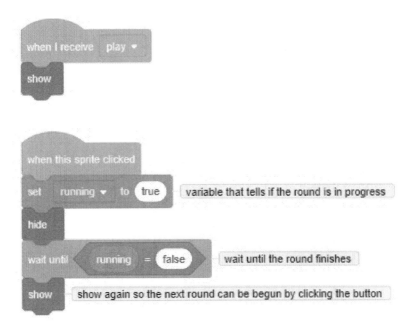

When a round starts, the enemies should be generated. The below Script is placed in the enemy Sprite for this purpose. However, assume the following first.

A list "waits" is for determining the wait time before the generation of the next enemy

A list of "types" is for telling the enemies beginning costumes when it's generated. A powerful enemy having more layers is made by the higher costume.

Into the list encode the boulder generation; that's an efficient programming part. Each "waits" list item is linked to the corresponding "types" list item. E.g., if "waits" item 1 is 4, then there is a wait of 4 secs by the enemy sprite before the creation of some enemy with costume # present in the "types" item 1. Moreover, by the blank list item, every round is separated. By the below Script, enemies are generated constantly, and there is a pause between round.

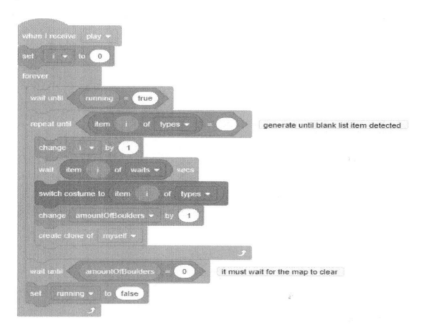

Enemies Programming

All the clones of the enemy have an easy way of determining the font. Four variables are there in association with the enemies.

- Progress

- Progress lead

- X lead

- Y lead

The progress variable is the private variable only. Each enemy progresses its own record. An enemy starts with 0 progress when it is generated. Along the path, with every moving pixel, the progress of it is added by 1. "Change y by () & update" block is made that moves the Sprite, and its progress is increased by it. Every enemy monitors the progress of itself constantly that whether it's bigger than the global variable "lead progress."

If the private progress of the enemy is bigger than the global variable lead progress. To its own, lead progress is set then, depicting the lead of it. Moreover, lead X & lead Y is set by the leading enemy to x & y position for identifying to the towers about the leading clone actual position.

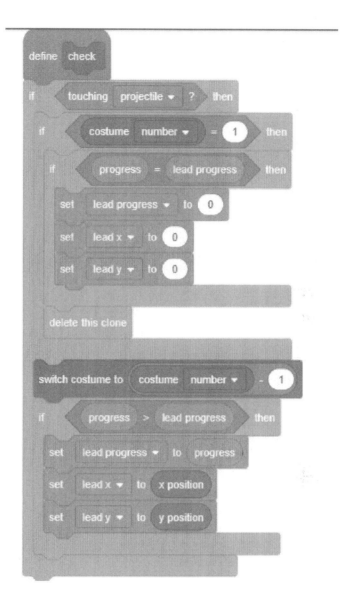

The tower game is now ready for playing. You can also try some new features for this game according to your liking. You should test some creative ideas further in this game.

Conclusion

Scratch is a howling but free source to help children and also adults to learn about coding without typing the code. Simply we can say that they can learn about structuring the code without the learning frustration of syntax also.

It is some sort of recreational work and has an enormous number of users. You can watch their projects and also copy it, that will be helpful for learning in a practical mode.

Though this is still coding, do not worry about if you do not remember a comma or brackets, as you have to do while performing the other languages. Developers chiefly designated the Scratch for kids having the age of 8 to 16 years. But parents with their young can enjoy it also.

The most interesting feature of scratch programming for children is learning in a simple way. It is not mandatory to be a genius in math, and no preceding preparation is required. It develops the entire programming skill by playing or practices. Here, playing and practicing is the vital component because the crux of the code looks like a bright unit. Hence the coding is entirely fun and amusing but still educational.

Printed by Amazon Italia Logistica S.r.l.
Torrazza Piemonte (TO), Italy

16839850R00098